TRAVELING BETWEEN THE LINES

Traveling Between the Lines
Europe in 1938

∾

The Trip Journal *of* John F. Randolph
and his Daughter's Response

Rebecca McBride

Rebecca McBride

For Lawanda and Sam,
Enjoy this journey
into history...

Epigraph Books
Rhinebeck, New York

Traveling Between The Lines: Europe in 1938 © 2010 by Rebecca McBride.
Photographs by John F. Randolph, 1938.

Library of Congress Control Number: 2010926815

ISBN: 978-0-9826441-2-6

Epigraph Books
27 Lamoree Road
Rhinebeck, New York 12572
USA 845-876-4861

Printed in the United States of America

CONTENTS

J OHN F. RANDOLPH earned his Ph.D. in mathematics
and astronomy from Cornell University in 1934 and
taught mathematics there until 1936. From 1936 to
1938, he was a member at the Institute for Advanced
Study in Princeton, New Jersey, in the School of Mathematics. Before returning to Cornell in September 1938
as assistant professor of mathematics, he and his wife,
Margaret, traveled in Europe. He kept a daily journal of
the trip from May 28 to September 1, 1938.

PREFACE

1. The Journal

I recognized the handwriting at once. It was small, precise, and surprisingly legible. Even at age 34, my father had a distinctive handwriting that hinted at his life as a mathematician. Growing up, I would see piles of paper with that same script but written in the language of formulas and fractions and arrows. There would be lots of white space on the page.

But here, in what I discovered was the first of four tiny notebooks, there was no white space. Instead, the writing starts at the top of the notebook's opening sheet and careens down the page and onto the next page without hesitation. At the end of the notebook are lists of items and their cost (pipe 5/6, liqueur 3/1, mints 1) and some names and addresses. I came across the notebooks in a carton of my father's papers long after his death in 1988.

First entry: "May 28, 1938. Got to Hook of Holland about 4 in the morning...." Was this a journal of the Black Forest cycling trip? I knew my parents had biked in Germany's Black Forest region at one time, but I knew little else. A lover of travel, I read on.

The more I read, the more I felt myself being pulled into the world of these little notebooks. It was as if the words in faded pencil drew me in to themselves and then placed me out into the world of 1938 Europe. Soon I could see that the notebooks were a record of my parents' trip abroad from May 28 to September 1, 1938, one year before the start of World War II.

I laid the notebooks out on my bed and began to read them, one by one. I couldn't stop. There I was, reading what my own father wrote, not for publication but as a record of my parents' daily life traveling in Holland, Belgium, Germany, Austria, Switzerland, France, England, and Wales. I was intrigued that I might learn how my father thought, felt, and acted as a young man before I ever knew him as my father. Maybe I might learn what my parents' marriage was like then.

Looking back to the 1930s, I was curious about why they were going on a vacation to Europe, and especially to Germany under the Nazis. I wondered how much my parents knew about the Nazi regime at that time.

I loved being transported to another world, but it took some effort to read the tiny, fading entries. A few weeks later, I decided to transcribe the notebooks. I merely wanted to be able to "see" the trip more easily. Once typed, the whole journal would become clear.

Then, however, I began to see things I hadn't noticed before. Suddenly the word "guilder" was shining up at me from the page. If I wanted to find out how much my parents paid to rent a bicycle in Holland, I needed to find out how much a guilder was worth at the time.

What about "lamp lighter"? On June 1, 1938, my father wrote, "About 9, we happened onto a lamp lighter making his rounds." The image of the lamp lighter at dusk was lovely, and I wondered, how much longer did the Belgian city of Bruges use gas lamps that were turned on individually?

So there began my pursuit. To find out about Dutch guilders and bicycles I looked online and in libraries but also wrote to a Dutch friend who quickly caught the bug of "that time, that place." He sent me photos of the Rotterdam train station and a typical Fongers bicycle in the thirties. He gave me a map of 1930s Europe when my husband and I visited him in The Hague in 2004.

As for the lamp lighter, I asked the Belgian Tourist Office in New York City about the use of gas lamps in Bruges. Ms. Opsomer replied that gas lamps were replaced by electric lights in 1920. I wrote to her again, quoting my father's reference to the lamp lighter, and asked her, "Are you sure?" She wrote back: "We returned with your concern to the city of Bruges and found that in the archives of the city a book (in Dutch) talks about the use of gas lanterns, and it seems that some gas lanterns were still in use until 1960. So, it seems that your dad was right after all."

And so it went, as I tracked down a few of my father's colleagues, some now in their nineties, and corresponded with people whose passion is biking in Europe or studying the history of ships or trains or mathematicians in Nazi Germany.

One of my happiest moments was finding a copy of the 1938 *Hand-Me-Down* guide from a used bookseller. *Hand-Me-Down* was published by the Student Tourist Class Association, Holland-America Line, during the thirties. Subtitled "the Student Guide of Europe," it started with Austria and ended with Yugoslavia, but—as if the authors couldn't help themselves—it also included entries for the Near East, Far East, and Africa. The description on the title page reads, "A book of hotels and restaurants and out-of-the-way places and little known things to do," personally recommended by student travelers. My parents consulted it conscientiously throughout their trip. When they couldn't find youth hostels, they often followed the guide's recommendations for places to stay.

But why did I do all of this? What compelled me to dig more and more deeply into my parents' experience?

My father enjoyed telling colorful, humorous stories about his childhood in Texas. My mother was much more private about hers in Lowell, Massachusetts. But any stories at all seemed to stop at the point of their marriage and adult life together. I enjoyed hearing the Texas stories but understood not to ask about my mother's family, and I don't remember asking many questions about their life before my brother and I were born.

As writer William Zinsser says, one of the saddest lines is, "I wish I had asked my mother, or my father, about that." At the last point I might have asked about their lives, including this trip to Europe, I didn't. When my mother died, I was 24 and giddy with freedom as a young adult going her own way, and when my father died, I was 43 and trying to cope as a single mother of two teenage sons. I wasn't thinking of asking my parents about their own lives.

The attention I give to my parents' trip in 1938 is the attention I give to their lives, now that they're gone. Journal in hand, I decided to follow their journey and through it learn more about them. I began writing back to my father the chronicler—writing to make the story whole. For the story in the notebooks is incomplete: my father's meticulous record, written as a travel log, only hints at my parents' life together early in their marriage and at a critical point in world history.

I yearned to know why my parents chose that time and place for their trip and what they saw and thought about when they were there. I began to read as much as I could about Europe in 1938 and in the years before and after. In hindsight, I see now what my parents did not know at the time or only partly knew.

It was too late to ask questions in person, but it wasn't too late to ask questions in writing, and to listen for the answers. I tried to fill in the empty spaces with the color of truth even if the truth is painful personally to me or historically. With what I learned along the way, I found a larger story, more whole, more real, of these two young adults—poor, newly married, traveling in pre-war Europe—who seven years later would be my parents.

2. To My Father

Your journal begins with your arrival in Holland on May 28, 1938. You, John, my father, and Margaret, my mother, are young, have little money, and are off on a great adventure. You travel by train, stay at youth hostels, rent bicycles, drink beer, climb mountains, and visit European mathematicians. This is the first of many trips abroad that you will take together.

But why Europe—why Germany and Austria—in 1938? Today, with all that is known about that time and those places, I want to ask, how much did you know about the world you were entering? I realize that the past has revealed itself gradually, like tide uncovering sharp edges of shells on a sandy beach, but still, what did you expect, and what did you find?

Reading your journal has led me to question, what did the American public know about Nazi Germany at this time, one year before the start of World War II? What did the media tell them? What did their government tell them? You have opened a door for me, your daughter, to your own past and to our country's history as well.

In entry after entry, you notice—and record—items like the prices of things, the rate of exchange, and the time of arrivals and departures. You are specific about the details of everyday life. Reading your journal, I learn the names of streets you walk, the cost of eggs and film, and changes in the weather from day to day.

What I don't know is how you feel as you travel together for three months, seeing things you had never seen before, in a Europe that was fast crumbling in on itself. I write to you to help myself learn.

Rebecca Randolph McBride

Note: The journal was transcribed word for word, with only a handful of spelling corrections. Text in parentheses is part of the journal; italicized text in parentheses contains my explanatory notes such as a translation or brief definition. Following the journal entries, I sometimes write directly to my father in italics; my writing to the reader, which generally contains historical background, is in regular font.

ACKNOWLEDGMENTS

This work has been years in the making, and throughout, I have received support from friends, family, and colleagues. My heartfelt gratitude goes first to my writers' group, Brin Quell, Ria Olsen, and Tomie Hahn, who have been with and for me every step of the way. Thalia Cassuto has been an enormous source of literary and practical inspiration. I treasure the hours spent with Elizabeth Stone on subtleties of language and approach. Lori Anderson-Moseman's creative input was priceless. Thanks also go to Joan Bloomberg and the late Dorothy Coxe for their contributions. Ismail Martens and Wolfgang Fritze helped me get started. John Rogers helped at the end.

I might not have completed this work without the tremendous support of the late Sanford L. Segal, my father's colleague at the University of Rochester, who provided both encouragement and information and was a personal connection to my father as well. I wish to thank Dr. Frank Mecklenburg, director of research at the Leo Baeck Institute, for his request to donate my father's journal and photographs to the Institute and to publish an early manuscript of this book on the Institute's digital archives. I am grateful for the opportunity.

I also want to thank the many individuals who responded so generously to my questions and requests for often obscure information. I am amazed at the helpfulness of people who do not know me—from staff and faculty at Cornell University, the Institute for Advanced Study, Oberlin College, and the University of Rochester, to those individuals working in historical societies and libraries.

Throughout, the steady encouragement of my husband, Farid, and my sons, Dennis and Nash, has meant everything to me.

EUROPE 1938

1

HOLLAND

The Dutch freighter John and Margaret Randolph took to Europe

Note: John and Margaret Randolph went by freighter to Europe with Rufus Oldenburger, who also had been a member at the Institute for Advanced Study the previous year, and another American, John Kludt. In his journal, John Randolph refers to them as M. (Margaret), R. (Rufus), and K. (Kludt).

May 28

Got to Hook of Holland about 4 in the morning and the pilot came aboard. The tide was against us so the Themisto (*a Dutch freighter*) could make only 6 or 7 knots all the way up the Maas (*River*) to Rotterdam.

The crew and officers were so excited they whistled, sang, and stomped around in their anxiety to get home.

The dikes along the river are all grown over with grass and the green looked very nice. Cattle grazed right down to the water.

Arrived in Rotterdam about 8 (time was set ahead 1 hour and 15 minutes). First, immigration officers came aboard, and then customs officers. It was 9 before we got away.

We startled the captain and officers by going ashore in the company's rowboat instead of taking the 35¢ water taxi. Even the members of the crew take the taxi.

The boats in the harbor surely made a sight. Flags from all countries.

Rufus,[1] M. (*Margaret*) and I carried our bags about 4 blocks and took a bus for uptown (Coolsingel). Left M. with bags while R. and I carried his bags to D. and P. station. Went back for M. and then to American Express. Got $4.00 worth of Holland money at rate of 1.8 guilders (or florins) per dollar and $5.00 in Belgium money at 30 francs for a dollar.[2]

John Kludt was shortchanged at the post office.

Kludt went with young Van der Ijk (*Van Eik or Van Eijk*) and got a good used bicycle (a Fongers—the best bic (*bike*) in Holland) for 19 guilders.[3]

After walking around in the crooked little streets, R., M. and I went to De Bijenkorf store (*the Beehive, a department store*) where R. bought shoes and a handkerchief and M. and I bought a towel and klompen (wooden shoes)—small ones.

K., M. and I are staying at the youth hostel (28 Oosterkade) (east quay).

Put R. on the train for Paris at 6:04. M. and I bought milk, apples, bread, and cheese and ate supper while standing in a doorway out of the rain.

Went to bed early.

How tremendously exciting it must be to finally arrive in Europe! You go by freighter so you probably slept hard the night before, until just before the sun rose over the North Atlantic. No jet lag for you.

On your first day you set the pattern of this trip. Arriving in Europe through the Hook van Holland (corner of Holland), by freighter, you take the free rowboat to shore rather than pay for the more convenient water taxi. You stay at the youth hostel. You notice—and record—items like prices, the rate of exchange, and the time of arrivals and departures.

In the journal, my father doesn't state where the voyage originated. Later he may have left a clue in a short story he wrote from the viewpoint of my then 11-year-old brother. In the story, my brother, as narrator, refers to his parents hitchhiking to Quebec to take a freighter to Europe. In the story there are 44 passengers and the trip lasts two weeks. "Poor Dad, he was sick all of the way."

In April 1938, President Roosevelt told the country in a fireside chat that another depression was on. In the short story, my brother says, "Dad finally got his thesis done and Mom typed it at night after working all day in the office. But then the depression came along and there were no jobs. They must have been pretty discouraged because Mom said, 'What the hell, let's go to Europe,' so they did."[4]

May 29

Last night besides K., M. and myself, there were the fellows from New York City, two Dutch boys, and a German girl.

For breakfast some bought from the hostel, but M. and I and some others ate our own at the same table—it seems to be the custom. Afterward everyone helps clean up.

Margaret used the "Mother's"[5] bicycle, K. his own, and I rented one for 60 cents for the day. We went northeast from Rotterdam on the road going along the top of a dike. Crossed Yssel (*or Ijssel*) River on a ferry (7 cents per person and bic) at Krimpen a/d (*aan de, on the*) Yssel and took a road following along the Krimpen a/d Lek river toward Schoonhoven and turned off at Amstel (*or Amstelveen*). There are many windmills, sometimes 200 or so very close together. This is Sunday and everyone is dressed up in their best. About a third of the men have their fancy klompen (wooden shoes) on, not just the plain wood, but carved and varnished a light tan or painted white. Whole families out walking together.

The houses are wonderful in their absolute cleanness and fresh paint. Windows are all decorated with woodcarving or painted glass. Nice colors in their paints; blue and red predominating. Flowers everywhere.

Margaret got very tired and kept going slower and slower. At Gouda she was so tired that she couldn't go on so we put her on the train for Rotterdam (Margaret 50 cents, bicycle 30 cents).

K. and I went on toward Rotterdam, but turned off to Zevenhuizen (*seven houses*) to look up an uncle of his. We found a man by the same name, but this man had no brother in America. No one could speak English and in the efforts to make ourselves understood we collected a larger and larger crowd. Finally someone remembered that the banker spoke English. He came, and although the uncle had left 40 years ago the banker remembered him well. The old uncle was dead and his son had moved to Rotterdam 15 years ago.

On the way in we stopped at a farmer's and bought two glasses of milk at 5 cents per. The farmer's evening milking was 64 liters.

M. got home all right and even ate supper at the hostel. We got in about 8.

Your friend John Kludt does what many Americans do in Europe—search for relatives that link them to the past. Reading your journal, I do that too.

You don't waste any time! I love the confidence with which you three young travelers set off on bicycles to explore the countryside on this your second day abroad. You see a lovely, bright countryside. Do you know about the Europe that lies beneath, waiting?

At this time, almost exactly two years before Germany's invasion of Holland, you are enjoying the still relaxed atmosphere and seeing the Dutch countryside through the eyes of tourists.

As shown in the file of Anne Frank's father, Otto Frank began trying to leave the Netherlands in 1938 and continued trying unsuccessfully after the Nazi occupation of that country. With hindsight, one might ask why he didn't try to emigrate earlier.

But he had already moved his family to Holland in 1933, and even after the occupation it seemed that Jews might escape the harsher realities of life in Germany. According to David Engel, Greenberg Professor of Holocaust Studies at New York University: "Neither Otto Frank nor anyone else could reasonably have predicted what would befall Jews in the Netherlands beginning in 1942."[6]

On May 25, 1938, Victor Klemperer, a professor in Dresden, Germany, wrote in his diary:

> Recently Heckmann, the gardener, and today Vogel, the grocer, in complete unanimity [said]: "I have no idea what's happening. I don't read a newspaper." People are apathetic and indifferent. In addition Vogel said: "It all seems like cinema to me." People simply regard it all as a theatrical sham, take nothing seriously and will be very surprised when the theater turns into bloody reality one day.[7]

Today we know the reality of events in May 1938. On May 28, Hitler met with his military commanders at the Reich Chancellery in Berlin and declared his "unshakeable will" to wipe Czechoslovakia "off the map."[8] The annexation of Austria in March 1938 was followed by the successful acquisition of the Sudetenland in Czechoslovakia in October. According to historian John Lukacs, "1938 was Hitler's year."[9]

May 30

Last night K. was sick and this morning was unable to go on. M. and I took the train for Amsterdam (round trip 2.60, one way was 1.90). Stopped at Delft and looked around but did not go in any of the buildings. A man on the street said that absolutely no one is allowed to go through the pottery and tile works. However, later the youth hostel Father said that if we had gone there they would have let us through.

At Amsterdam we had lunch and went to the Rijksmuseum (*national museum*) where M. explained a lot about the old Dutch painters to me.

The wind was very strong so walking around was unpleasant. Thus we saw very little else.

We returned to Rotterdam in time for dinner at 6:30. K. had been in bed all day but was feeling better.

After dinner I took a walk along the Maas River across from where the New Amsterdam was docked.[10] By accident I returned by way of Schedmaashe Dijk (dike) just when all the crowds were beginning to go into the halls and the girls were taking their places at corners and dark doorways.

Your education in West Texas may not have included seventeenth century Dutch painters, but you are willing to learn about them from your young wife. Later, Margaret will explain "a lot about the old Dutch painters" to me too. She will show me the light from the window in The Cook by Jan Vermeer and the detail in The Moneylender and His Wife by Quentin Massys.

In the summer of 1961, as my father stayed home to teach and write, my mother and I spent a rare month together in Europe. She led me—a rebellious teenager—through the Louvre, the Jeu de Paume, and the Uffizi, and into gardens, cathedrals, and Roman amphitheatres. Traveling to London, Paris, Amsterdam, Venice, and Florence, we stayed in small hotels or pensions with the toilet down the hall and many stairs to climb. Gradually I relaxed into the trip, and the two of us ended up enjoying one another's company and the sights.

I kept my mother's art history books after she died in 1970. In one of them, *Masterpieces of Painting* (National Gallery of Art,

Washington, D.C., 1946), I found a folded, yellowed newspaper clipping (*New York Herald Tribune*, November 21, 1937) with articles on art exhibits in Europe and the United States. Perhaps she was preparing for this trip abroad. One article was entitled "A German Modern":

> At the Nierendorf Gallery (in New York City), paintings by Karl Hofer are shown, including canvases of 1934 to 1937. This German modern, who models with "light" and color, and gains a bold expressiveness in the process, is now taboo in Germany. Thus America, which has already responded with appreciation of him, has the choice of his works. One of the best here is a bold "Sunflower," another the "Nude" with arms folded, which has a curious affinity with Gothic sculpture.

Did my mother know why Karl Hofer was taboo in Germany in November 1937? Did she know that 12 days before this article appeared (November 8, 1937), a large anti-Jewish exhibition opened at Munich's Deutsches Museum?[11]

Karl Hofer was a German painter, draughtsman, and printmaker, who was dismissed from his teaching post by the Nazis in 1934 and forbidden to paint or exhibit his work. In July 1937, his "Seated Nude on Blue Cushion" had been seized by the Nazis and included in their exhibit of "Degenerate Art" in Munich.[12] He and his brother Josef owned the Galerie Nierendorf in Berlin, but the gallery was given notice to stop exhibiting altogether ("quit the rooms") by summer 1938.[13]

In 1936, Karl Hofer opened a second Nierendorf gallery in New York City to exhibit German artists—hence the exhibit in November 1937 of his work. The NYC gallery remained open until 1946. Today, the Nierendorf gallery is operating again in Berlin, at Hardenbergstraße 19.

NOTES

1. Rufus Oldenburger was a mathematician (Ph.D. 1934, University of Chicago) who also had been at the Institute for Advanced Study in Princeton the previous year.

2. In 2003, before the Euro was adopted, the rate was .86 Dutch guilders to a dollar and one Belgian franc to a dollar.

3. A well-known Dutch company that used high-quality engineering details, Fongers made reliable and elegant bicycles.

4. John F. Randolph's Ph.D. thesis, Carathéodory Measure and a Generalization of the Gauss-Green Lemma, was actually completed in September 1934.

5. It was common for the couples who ran youth hostels to be called Mother and Father. This was part of an attempt to make the hostels feel more like home for young travelers.

6. Yivo Institute for Jewish Research. "Otto Frank File Found at YIVO." Press Release, February 14, 2007.

7. Klemperer, I Will Bear Witness, 1933-1941: A Diary of the Nazi Years, 258-9.

8. Parssinen. The Oster Conspiracy of 1938, 38.

9. Lukacs, Five Days in London: May 1940, 9.

10. This grand ocean liner must have been poised to depart on her first voyage. A 1938 pamphlet from the Holland-America Line stated: "Completed by the Holland-America Line in May, 1938 for the North Atlantic trade, the S.S. Nieuw Amsterdam was one of the last vessels built with "old world" tastes in interior decor and comforts. The ship's trans-Atlantic career was cut short by the outbreak of World War II during which she was operated by the British government as a troop transport. Following the war and after extensive refitting, the Nieuw Amsterdam embarked on a long and successful career as a passenger liner in both trans-Atlantic and cruise service." Printed with permission. Richard O. Aichele, Information Works, Inc., P.O. Box 4725, Saratoga Springs, NY 12866. www.inforworks.com

11. Friedlander, Nazi Germany and the Jews: Vol. 1. The Years of Persecution, 1933-1939, 253.

12. Holocaust Claims Processing Office, New York State Banking Department, "Paintings Returned to Heirs of Holocaust Victims." Press Release, November 17, 2001.

13. Galerie Nierendorf website: www.nierendorf.com

2

Belgium

May 31

Got up at 7, rushed around and left in time to catch the 8:20 train for Esschen (*Essen*). K. was better this morning. At the border the customs officer had me open my bag but disturbed nothing and did not even look at Margaret's. We had already bought tickets from Esschen—Antwerp—Brussels (Bruxelles)—Bruges. Did not stop at Antwerp.

At Brussels we stayed four hours. Had lunch in a place listed in the Hand-Me-Down[1] but their prices had gone up. The place listed for laces was very good though, and M. bought some handkerchiefs and a doily.[2] Went into another lace place but were disgusted with their high pressure salesmanship. Saw the Grande Place and were impressed by the old buildings, 1402, 1454, etc.

Also saw the "Manneken-Pis" but there were salesgirls standing in shop doors in the neighborhood making little "mannekens" "pis" all over the sidewalk.[3]

Got back to the station to find that there is a 15 minute difference between Belgium and Holland time. Luckily, Belgium time is slower so we only had to wait 15 minutes instead of missing the train.[4]

Arrived in Brugge (*Bruges*) about 5. We had picked out the Tower Bridge Pension from the Hand-Me-Down as a likely place to stay.[5] Go out of station, turn left, walk by taxi stand to train waiting station. Take car 4 and get off at Place Memling, walk to the left 100 yards (I mean 30 meters or so), you cross a canal and there you are. It is a wonderful place. For 70 Bf (*Belgian francs*) two people get a wonderful room and even more wonderful meals.[6]

After supper we walked around and were absolutely thrilled to death. The old buildings, narrow streets, beautiful canals took our hearts away. Not just a few interesting places; everything is so unexpected and charming. We are sorry we stayed so long in Rotterdam and are already talking of staying an extra day.

Is this the last of John Kludt? It appears that you leave him behind, feeling better, in Rotterdam. "...everything is so unexpected and charming." Isn't that the best experience one can have while traveling!

In June of 2004, sixty-six years later, my husband, Farid, and I also traveled by train from Brussels to Bruges. We were on vacation, traveling in Belgium and France, seeing old friends and enjoying the sights. But for me, going to Bruges was important for another reason: I wanted to experience this beautiful city that my parents responded to with such pleasure in 1938. My father was so precise in his description of where they stayed and what they did that I felt I had a chance to follow them around for a few days.

After settling in at our bed and breakfast, we searched for the name of the street where they stayed—Pont de la Tour—on the town map but couldn't find it. A man at the tourist office frowned when I showed him the address from the *Hand-Me-Down* guidebook—1 Pont de la Tour. "No, no," he said with a wave of his arm, sweeping aside the past, "we have no longer French, only Flemish. French, that is no more."

After a long history of friction between Flemish-speaking Flanders and its French-speaking rulers, this northern region of Belgium returned to its Flemish roots in the years after World War II. Now French is primarily spoken in the southern region of Belgium known as Wallonia.

It is odd that my father used the Flemish name, Brugge, in his journal, even though the rest of the place names he cited are French. Today, Americans use the French name, Bruges, even though the rest of the place names we use are Flemish.

Overhearing our conversation, a woman at the tourist office said, "Yes, there used to be a pension there, and there is a hotel nearby." So we followed my father's directions to the Tower Bridge Pension, walking on old brick-covered streets, past the preserved stone houses with their quirky gable windows and red-tiled roofs. We found the square with the statue of Hans Memling, the fifteenth century painter, then, following one of the small streets off the square, we arrived at a bridge over a canal. The sign on the bridge read Toren Brug (Tower Bridge).

A woman passing by asked us in French (ironically) if we needed help and told us there is a hotel around the corner. We found the hotel sign with the customary Bruges lantern on the wall by the front door. The concierge, alone behind the counter in the dark lobby, was happy to have our unexpected company. When I inquired about the pension, he raised his hand, saying "Wait," and pulled out a history of the hotel from a nearby shelf. The hotel housed German soldiers during the occupation but had never been a pension.

Walking back toward the bridge, we saw it—Number 1, but no longer a pension. How did we miss it? Perhaps we were looking too hard. I took a picture of the white building on the edge of the canal, right near the bridge. I could see them both, my young parents, stepping out of the door to walk the medieval streets of Bruges.

June 1

Got up late this morning. Looked out of the window, and there just a few yards (meters) away was a regular honest-to-goodness market. After breakfast we strolled through the market. You can buy everything—groceries, vegetables, leather goods, clothing, cloth, lace, fur, etc., etc. Most of the things were not of high quality but the saleswomen did not make an effort to sell things; you could look as long and as leisurely as you wanted to.

We walked on to Walplein where there are several women sitting in their doorways making lace, and incidentally selling their handkerchiefs. They will have as many as 40 bobbins that they throw around in a seemingly haphazard manner, but by sticking pins here, there, and everywhere, a strip of lace gets longer. Saw one piece of lace being made with 350 bobbins.

Had to rush back in time to eat at 12:30.

Took two shirts to have laundered. They will cost 2.25 Bf apiece (i.e., 7 ½ cents). Lunch: veal meat balls, cauliflower, boiled potatoes, grease gravy, and apple for dessert. Dinner: soup, fresh shrimp and tomatoes with horseradish mayonnaise, breaded veal cutlet (large), lettuce salad, creamy mashed potatoes, prunes (may not sound good for dessert, but they were wonderful).

This afternoon went a winding route roughly following a canal to the station and looked up schedules and rates for the trip to the German border. Next went back of the station to the Grand Canal, along the canal a distance through the Beguinage (*spiritual community*) and then to the church St. "Sauveur" (*Sint-Salvatorskathedraal*), passed the Grand Place (*now the Markt*), and home.

This evening we walked to the left from Tower Bridge in more of a workingmen's section. Little shops had klompen in the windows. M. later bought two little bells at 4 Bf. Passed the Prinsenhof (*house of the Prince, or palace, where Maria van Bourgondie, daughter of Karel de Stoute—Charles the Bold— lived*) and then home very foot weary and to bed at 10:30.

About 9 we happened onto a lamp lighter going his rounds. Most of the streets are well lit by gas lamps that have to be turned on individually.

On our second day in Bruges, Farid and I explored the city and visited the Kantcentrum (lace center), with its small rooms, formerly fifteenth century almshouses. We learned that bobbin lace making was a technique developed in Flanders in the sixteenth century. Threads of silk, linen, or cotton on numerous bobbins are crossed and braided around a framework of pins.

I returned in the afternoon to watch a demonstration of lace making. Most of the women were working slowly. But a woman in the corner by herself was making lace exactly as my father describes, throwing the bobbins back and forth so quickly and expertly that I found myself staring at her hands. She did not acknowledge me. Only after sitting there for twenty minutes or so did I catch the barest brush of a glance in my direction from the corner lace maker.

June 2

This morning we started out at 10:30, went to Belfry (*clock tower*) (first reading a pamphlet in the information room). Entrance 2 Bf. The tower was first built in 1248 and later added to in 1616. The height is 220 feet.

The quarter hour chimes are played automatically by a giant music box, the drum is 6 feet in diameter, and 15 feet long. The pegs are screwed into square holes. The drum goes once around each hour, the chimes for time on the hour taking 3/4 of the drum. We were standing at the big bell when it struck 12. Tunes are changed every two years. Today the bell master was in the tower helping change the small bells which are slightly out of tune with the large ones.

This afternoon we changed $13 into Belgian francs @ 29.3, down a little.

Went to the Gruuthusemuseum.[7] The building is part of a baronial residence erected about 1465. Many old pieces of furniture, kitchen utensils, swords, armor, etc. and a collection of lace, one broad and very delicate piece said to have taken three years to make each yard. Price of admission 3 francs.

Bought three more bells. Got some apples and other food for lunch tomorrow. After supper paid bill of 202.75 + 10% = 222.75 Bf (*approximately $7.00 for three nights*). This includes a 1 Bf tax per person for the night.

Went for a short walk and timed ourselves from station home so we would know how much time to allow, and decided to be called at 7:30 instead of 8.

There was a military band concert in the Grand Place, and we listened to two numbers. M. saw a piece of tapestry in the window for 6 BF and decided to stop and get it in the morning.

You certainly are "called" to be a mathematician. Numbers are so important to you. On this trip, during a period of economic depression, do you record prices so precisely because you want to keep track of expenses?

But I feel that it's more than that. You like knowing the height of the Belfry, the diameter and length of the drum, the exact dates of construction, as well as the current rate of exchange, and how much it has changed since the day before. An artist would describe the tower in terms of its architectural details. A photogra-

pher would compare the light and shadow at different times of day. You describe through numbers.

In 2004, Farid and I also visited the Belfort-Hallen (Bell Tower and Covered Market)— the Belfry—situated on the southeastern corner of the city's large square, the Markt. Dominating Bruges, the bell tower is so high that I could not capture it in one photograph. My *Berlitz Pocket Guide* describes the Hallen as a "magnificent complex of brick buildings" which in the Middle Ages would have been "crammed with traders, the air heavy with the scent of spices brought by Venetian merchants." The 47-bell carillon still rings out throughout the day.

But I am confused by your numbers. You say the pamphlet states the tower was first built in 1248 and added to in 1616. The pamphlet we see when we visit in 2004 gives the dates of 1742–48, probably the dates of completion. The website I consult, www. trabel.com/brugge, gives different dates: 1240, beginning of construction, added to in 1482–86 after a fire, and another fire in 1741. There's more confusion about the height: You say 220 feet, my pocket guide says 300 feet (90 meters), and the current pamphlet says 83 meters (272 feet).

I throw up my hands at this proliferation of numbers, just as I did as a girl studying arithmetic. My father tried to interest me in the beauty and challenge of mathematics, but it was no use. I was easily frustrated by numbers, formulas, geometric shapes, and the use of "x." It all made no sense at a time when words spoke to me so effortlessly.

In any case, my parents clearly enjoyed their time in Bruges in May 1938. Two years later, on May 10, 1940, the Nazis invaded Belgium, France, Holland, and Luxembourg. William L. Shirer broadcast from Berlin, "The decisive battle of the war has begun." Whether my parents felt any foreboding of the war to come, I will never know.

Also on May 10, 1940, Neville Chamberlain resigned as Britain's prime minister, and Winston Churchill, who had been a lone voice warning against the dangers of Nazism, took his place. On May 28, 1940, Belgium's King Leopold II ordered his armies to surrender to Hitler.

NOTES

1. *Hand-Me-Down: The Student Guide of Europe* was published by the Student Tourist Class Association, Holland-America Line, during the 1930s. The section for each country contains advice on places to stay, eat, and visit by town or city. All of the entries were submitted by student travelers, and many are whimsical and off-beat. The guide began in 1927 with several hundred students pooling their "pet discoveries" to pass them on to other students so they could "save their pocketbooks" and enrich their trips with "tidbits of information that one usually unearths too late." Only 2,000 copies of the 1938 edition were printed.

2. "Beware of imitations in lace shops selling imitation lace . . . especially those near the Cathedral and those to which you are taken on sight-seeing tours." *Hand-Me-Down*, 1938.

3. Manneken-Pis is a statue of a little boy making a "fountain" dating from 1619. Supposedly, he saved Town Hall by extinguishing a sputtering bomb.

4. Brussels is 1/60th of a degree to the west of Amsterdam, making it 15 minutes earlier at that time. The Dutch and Belgians have been in the same time zone since 1940.

5. "Tower Bridge, 1 Pont de la Tour . . . quiet, clean, comf., charming English spoken . . . exc. food . . . pens (*pension*) 35 Bfrs." *Hand-Me-Down*, 1938.

6. One Belgian franc was worth 3.4 cents, so the cost of staying one night for two was $2.38

7. Gruuthusemuseum, a palace of the Lords of Gruuthuse, was a farm that had a monopoly on the sale of gruut, an herb and spice mixture used to flavor beer.

3

GERMANY

June 3

We're called at 7:30. After breakfast I took the bags and went by train to the station and M. walked to get my shirts from the laundry and the tapestry she saw last night.

Train to Brussels (Midi) and to station Nord by tram. Had a little time to look around. Train to Liège and changed. First German town was Aachen. Customs and immigration officers very nice. Arrived at Köln (*Cologne*) at 4. Asked a storm trooper about the Jugendherbergen (*youth hostels*) but did not get along so well (*i.e., speaking German*). He took us to a policeman in front of the station who helped us some.

Cashed some travel marks and walked over bridge carrying bags to the hostel. Had considerable trouble because no one there knew much more English than I knew German.

After supper (a lot of potato salad, roll, 2 soft boiled eggs and a bottle of milk (.78 RM) (*Reichsmarks*),[1] we walked back over bridge around Cathedral (started in 1248) and M. looked for shops with Eau de Cologne, and later we looked in windows at cameras. Back to hostel just before closing time (9:30) and to bed.

I notice you have no trouble getting into Germany. You and Margaret are a young American couple on vacation, and Aachen is simply the gateway to Germany.

By June of 1938, Nazi persecution of German Jews has reached an unimaginable degree. From Hitler's rise to power in 1933 on, the process of "Aryanization" has become institutionalized throughout German government and daily life, clearing the way for the eventual Holocaust after November 1938. How

*much do you know about this? This question lies in wait through-
out my reading of your journal. It bubbles up to the surface as you
enter Germany.*

In the early thirties, Aachen had one of the largest Jewish com-
munities (more than a thousand residents) in the Rhineland,
with many merchants and professionals, mostly integrated into
the life of the city. In Aachen, there was early local resistance
to the Nazis and even a rare demonstration in support of the
Jews after the general, one-day boycott of Jewish shops on
April 1, 1933, ordered by Hitler.[2] The boycott, which ironically
took place on a Saturday, was largely a failure since Germans
ignored it and many Jewish shops were already closed for the
Sabbath.

Two years later, Aachen would become a setting for battle
when the Nazis attacked Belgium in May 1940. In November 1944, American and German troops fought house-to-
house for the town. After the war, Aachen had only 62 Jewish
residents.[3] As for Cologne, starting in March 1942, the city was
bombed hundreds of times and by the end of the war was almost totally destroyed.

June 4

The hostel is full of youngsters, a good many about 10 and
from there on up to 20 with very few older. About four times
as many boys as girls. They certainly are a healthy husky lot.
The boys all in shorts with uniform type of shirts, and each
with a knife at his belt and a small pack. Each girl also has a
pack. Some are walking but most of them have bicycles.

The room I slept in last night had 30 double-decker beds,
most of them occupied so there were nearly 60 there. There
must have been five such rooms occupied by boys last night.
We were called at 5:30 this morning. Breakfast at the hostel.

After taking our bags to the station we started looking for a camera and bought one in the third place we looked.

Took train from Köln at 10:37 for Koblenz. The two hour stay in Koblenz we spent walking down the Rhine to the mouth of the Mosel. Also had lunch of fish and potatoes at .35.

The trip up the Rhine from Koblenz to Bingen was wonderful. Much to our surprise the boat was not overly crowded. The day was perfect, nice and warm, practically no clouds and a clear atmosphere. The hills with their terraced vineyards are different from anything I have ever seen. Each little town is a picture with its castle lording over it. To describe each would be laborious and to remember them impossible.

Took our first picture with the Leica at St. Goar. M. with St. G. in background. A woman from N.J. took a picture of M. and me as we passed the Lorelei (*a sheer slate cliff*).

Arrived Bingen at 19 o'clock so took ferry (*across the Rhine*) immediately for Rudesheim. I started to carry the bags to the youth hostel but found that it was away up a hill out of town at least half a mile.[4] We then took the bags back to the station and checked them after putting the things necessary for the night in the knapsack. Then since it was so late we looked for a room in town. The one we found furnished real atmosphere, so much so that M. almost refused to stay. We were given two keys—one to the room and the other (*drawing of key here*) to the gate from a lower courtyard to the street. A circular stair led from a little old door to our attic floor. Our room was a wonder, but nice and clean. From our window we looked out on terraced vineyards that came right up to the trees next to the house. We were given a flash light to pilot ourselves through the dark stair ways and halls on our return after dark.

This being a holiday (Pentecost)[5] all of the prominent restaurants and taverns were full. However, we found a quiet little hotel and had a fair meal of ham, eggs, potatoes, bread, butter and a bottle of Rhine wine, all for 4.30. The wine was made by the proprietor of the hotel. A very cute little waitress.

After eating we walked around and hearing loud music and singing in a place we went in. It was a regular wine hall crowded to the limit, but they found us two seats. We took a small bottle of wine (1.85) and danced on a 2 by 4 space with about 12 other couples. Lots of fun. The other couple at our table was from Berlin and I had fun trying to talk German to them above the din of the music, singing, and talking. Got to bed about 11:30 dead tired.

Arriving in Germany, you look for a camera, and the next day you buy one. You must have planned to buy a Leica standard model with focal plane shutter with speeds from 1/20th to 1/500th seconds. I learn these details from a handwritten record you make of the purchase: $81 plus costs for accessories. According to your Leica manual, "the Leica camera, which was presented to the world shortly after the World War, is today the Number One camera of our modern times." A photographer friend of mine thinks you are "very hip" to buy a Leica in Germany.

From my experience growing up with you both, I am surprised that you go to a nightspot with loud music. But in 1938, you two are young and want to dance. What a happy picture of the two of you dancing in that tiny space.

This is your first full day in Germany. Reading your entry, one would never know that for some of its citizens this is a country in turmoil. The scenery is gorgeous, the people friendly, the spirit one of holiday.

June 5

This morning we were lazy and got out late. Had breakfast in the room. Took a picture of M. under the big feather bed.

Walked out of town a little way and went off of the road a little way in a vineyard. It was up a hill back of town. Looking down on Rudesheim and across the Rhine to Bingen made a very nice sight.

Thought of stopping at Wiesbaden on the way to Frankfurt but because of lack of time did not. At Frankfurt we checked bags and after trying to find when the train goes to Heidelberg, walked to the Römer or old town hall. Had a glass of beer before going in. Stayed in the Römer so long that we missed our train.

When we got to the station to take the next train I found that what I thought was the time of departure from Frankfurt was the time of arrival in Heidelberg. We had to wait 1 hour 20 minutes for the next train.

This train was one of the Extra Special (called D-Zug) (*the fastest steam train at the time*) trains. The third class cars were nicely upholstered, clean, toilet clean and hand towels furnished.

Arrived in Heidelberg at 8 but it was 9 before we got to the youth hostel only to find it full. Went back to Bismarck Platz and left M. with bags while I went to find the Pension (found in Hand-Me-Down) run by Frau Tinkle. It was raining and dark when I finally found the place. I had to holler my poor German from across the street to a woman up five stories, and all I learned was that "Frau Tinkle ist gestorbt (*has died*)."

After trying many places I finally thought of going to the Zimmernachweis (*tourist office/information*). There they told me that the only rooms they knew of were at the Europäischer Hof (the best hotel in town). In the end I took these, 2 single rooms at 4.50 RM each + 15%.

You get to see the Römer, with its famous gables marking the city hall since 1405, and the city of Frankfurt itself before it is bombed by the Allies in 1944. It is good, I think, that you enjoy your visit there so much that you miss the train.

Your Hand-Me-Down guide lists Frau Tinkle's pension in Heidelberg as a bed and breakfast with free baths and a balcony but says it is not attractive from the outside. What attracts you must be the price: 2.50 RM.

The guide describes the Europäischer Hof as having a "charming, lovely garden, excellent service, dancing." Frommer's Germany 2010 guide calls it by far the most glamorous of Heidelberg's hotels with its Oriental rugs and spa, and puts it in the "very expensive" category ($600 for a double room). So, at the exchange rate of 1 RM = .40, instead of paying $1 for a room, you end up paying more than $4. Heidelberg is filled with visitors, and you are forced to live in luxury for a change, at least for one night. How unusual for a young couple traveling on a shoestring!

In 1934, another youthful traveler, the American writer Wright Morris, found himself in Heidelberg:

Yet at the open casement window in Heidelberg, along with the keen pleasures of expectation, I registered my first presentiments that something was rotten in this picture of perfection. Behind the light and the shadow, the trilling voices of the children, lurked a danger in which we were all complicit. Was it strange that I should feel this so intensely in Heidelberg?

It was heavenly weather. On the bridge over the Neckar I stood long and long, looking at the castle, my fancy on the Rhine Maidens in the mists behind it. On the posters in the streets of Heidelberg I read that Germany, too, had a depression. The faces of the unemployed stared at me from the billboards. Most of the young I saw in the streets, however, were dressed in some sort of uniform, and seemed buoyant and assured, striding about like *Wandervögel*[6] into the future.[7]

June 6

The morning was nice and bright. All the people and all the swastikas were out in full color. After eating breakfast in the room M. sat under the trees at a nice little table and wrote letters while I took the bags to the youth hostel and got beds for the night (some come down) (*fold down from the wall*).

We went to old Heidelberg University and visited the old prison and the new building. The new building is nothing to see in Heidelberg. Next went to castle and went on one of their regular conducted tours of the castle. Met the women from N.J. that we saw on the Rhine boat.

Still great crowds at the hostel and the boys were noisy so I did not get to sleep until late.

I want to know what you think about the swastika in June 1938. It seems that as a visitor to Germany, you see it as simply the national flag at the time.[8]

All citizens were supposed to display the flag, but Jews were forbidden to do so by the Nuremberg Laws. As a result, for some "mixed" families (still considered citizens), deciding whether to hang the swastika outside the front door was fraught with anxiety.[9]

Street in Heidelberg

June 7

Started out early to look for bicycles to rent. Went to four different shops and finally found some fine bicycles. M.'s is an "Ideal" and mine a "Diplomat." They go very easily, so easy in fact that M. thought we were going down hill all of the time whereas we were going up the Neckar.

Started from the bicycle shop in Heidelberg at 11:14 and got to Mosbach (60 km = 36 miles) at 7:00.

Took some pictures along the way. Just after taking one picture a motorcycle policeman came by and told us that from the next village (Zwingenberg) to Stuttgart no picture taking was allowed.

At Neckarelz just two miles from Mosbach M. took a nasty spill. Skinned her knee badly. It will be sore tomorrow.

The hostel is a little out of town but nicely located in a valley. The house is an old farm house with barns attached.

Margaret resting by the Neckar River

After washing up we found that no supper was left so walked into town and had supper at the Prince Carl on the recommendation of the Father.

There was a fire in town and they were winding up the hose when we went by on the way home. The fanciest firemen I ever saw and 35 of them. Dark blue uniform, with red trimmings, silver buttons, wide leather belts some with swords slung to them, high leather boots, and black helmets with a silver ridge from brow to back of neck. Even the fire hose was colorful, a bright orange. The hook and ladder wagon, hose wagon, and water pump were all two wheeled carts pushed by the fancy men. Lots of fun.

It may be that on the road between Zwingenberg and Stuttgart, you are not allowed to take pictures because there is a military factory or even an army post.

In his memoir about growing up in Germany in the 1930s, Henry Metelmann writing about Germany's secret armament program, remembers the Ottensener Eisenwerke (Iron Works), a large factory complex employing hundreds of workers in his neighborhood. It was rumored that the workers were producing military hardware since no one was allowed in without being checked at the main gates. Eventually, "the truth came out into the open, for on every working day at a certain hour in the early afternoon we children waited at the gate to watch one cannon, hooked on to the back of a military lorry, come rolling out."[10]

June 8

The left pedal of my bic (*bike*) needed fixing at the shop this morning. Fixing pedal and oil can with oil 50 p. (*Pfennige; 1 Reichsmark = 100 Pfennige*). Also M.'s knee needed fixing. Fixing knee .39. Got ½ liter of milk apiece in a little shop and stood there eating our own rolls and marmalade and had a nice talk with the proprietor and his wife. Later took a picture of him and his little corner. Altogether did not get started until 10:40.

Went off of road a little to see Bad-Wimpfen where we rode around the little town up on a hill, interesting and a nice view of the valley. Sent card to Canadian Travel League. Bought two glasses of beer and sat there drinking beer and eating our own rolls and cheese.

Stopped at the youth hostel at Heilbronn early, 4:30. Had a good shower bath. Had supper at a regular German working man's place, the Kaffee and Speisehaus (*eating house*) on Über Neckarstrasse. Soup (keep the bowl for the rest of the meal), sauerbraten with lots of gravy, gemischter (*mixed*) salat (potatoes and lettuce). First cut up the meat (in the soup bowl), put on half of the Spaetzle (*homemade pasta*), then half of the salat, then half of the gravy, mix all together and then eat. Repeat with other half. Also had ½ liter Most (new wine), no good.

To bed early.

I notice you send a card to the Canadian Travel League. Are you already trying to arrange passage home? Are you worried about being able to get back to the States?

The Canadian Travel League was a company specializing in freighter travel from Montreal and Quebec to Rotterdam, Antwerp, and other ports in Europe. In *Vagabond Voyaging: The Story of Freighter Travel,* published in 1938, Larry Nixon lists the cost of sailing to Belgium and Holland as $75 one way, and $145 round trip. The company was responsible for arranging bookings and handling passports and other details for its passengers.

Acknowledging that low cost is the main attraction for travelers who want to see the world, Nixon enthusiastically lists many other benefits and charms of freighter travel: you are thrown into close contact with the officers of the ship, you meet other adventurous, interesting travelers ("authors, writers, artists, and college professors"), and you get to avoid the social and dress demands of a passenger liner (you find "slacks and sweaters rather than tails and evening gowns"). He writes: "Rates and romance have their appeal, but there's another important factor, one that probably moves most tramp trippers to take their second journey: the absolute freedom for the passenger, the absence of pretense, show-off, or fol-de-rol."[11]

June 9

This morning oiled and tightened screws on bics. Were away to our earliest start. The weather is very hot. Had lunch in a regular beer garden and ate our own rolls and wurst. Many more hills than yesterday and have to push up some of them. This afternoon slept ½ hour. At Stuttgart took picture of M. and 3 BDM girls (*Bund Deutscher Mädel—League of German Girls*).[12] ½ liter of beer apiece in Stuttgart.

Margaret, second from left, with BDM girls

From Stuttgart to Tübingen is 39 km. with no youth hostel between, but we decided to go anyway. There is an extremely long hill going out of Stuttgart and we had to walk three miles pushing the bics. From then on it was a series of long hills up and long coasts down. Stopped in a little village for supper in a regular country inn. There were five girls from about 12–18 (*years old*) there drinking beer.

They evidently had been working in the fields all day. The owner of the place was also in work clothes and seemed to be the girls' boss. We had a lot of fun talking (or trying to talk) to the people there. Four men came in later.

From where we ate to Tübingen is 20 km. About three up, three down, three up, and then 11 down (we hardly had to pump a single time on this stretch). The sun went down in a very pretty sunset as we pushed up the first hill. The moon was about half full and was very pretty as the road wound through dense forest of rather tall pine. Toward the last of the long hill it got quite dark and my flash light came in handy.

You are such a good photographer! I really like this picture of my young mother and the three BDM girls, all looking healthy, happy, and carefree. Their smiling faces show the natural light of youth. The girl on the right wears the BDM costume of dark blue skirt, white blouse, and tie. Perhaps these three are participating in the BDM program of working in the country as farm hands or in the farmer's house, or as maids in households.

I find it so tragic that the young people in Nazi Germany were enlisted to advance Hitler's racist cause through organizations set up for youth—the BDM for girls and Hitler Jugend (Hitler Youth) for boys. Your photograph arouses such mixed feelings in me: here you are socializing with a group that supported the Nazis and yet, I can see that these are three young women who probably couldn't care less about politics and are simply enjoying your company.

Henry Metelmann was an enthusiastic member of the Hitler Jugend for six years in the thirties despite his father's desperate attempts to make him see that he was being brainwashed by the Nazis:. "I was so elated, so proud of being a German."[13] He remembers that he learned discipline, competitive sports, games, military maneuvers, marches, songs, and positive German "history"—designed to instill in the youth a fervent, unconditional love for the Fatherland. For the young Metelmann the indoctrination worked all too well until, too late, he came to understand his father's deep misgivings. His father died before the war was over.

A year later, in March 1939, joining the Hitler Youth will be mandatory. When it became public in 2005 that Joseph Ratzinger, who would become Pope Benedict XVI, joined in 1941 when he was 14, this was his defense—that he had no choice.

June 10

Of all things, we had a private room in a house of the Hitler Jugend and even so paid only one RM for two of us. The room had two very nice cots, two little stands, a table, a chair, a large clothes chest, and a telephone. Very nicely furnished with painted walls and ceilings (white), hard wood floors, and large window. The whole hostel was especially built in 1935 and is modern and nice in every way.

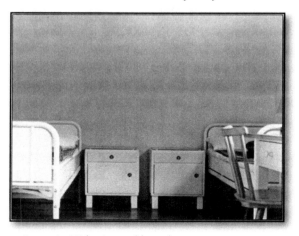

Room in Hitler Jugend hostel

Last night a rather heavy rain fell, and this morning it was still sprinkling. In a let-up we started out and after mailing post cards at the Post Office went to the University. Professor Knopp (*Konrad Knopp*)[14] was not there at first, but rain held us in the building (a very modern one) for some time and I got to see him before we left (at about 11:30). He is much younger than I expected to find him.

Out of town a short distance it started to sprinkle again, and we went under some heavy trees for a time. After it let up a little we put on our top coats and started on. Seeing a farm shed open close to the road, we went in. The farmers had so much to sell so we ate a lunch of rolls, cheese, and water. I missed a darned good chance to get a picture of two little German girls blowing soap bubbles.

At Balingen we started on, but turned back, only to find that the youth hostel has no accommodations for girls. However, the Gasthaus next door has rooms for .80 M. apiece, so we both stayed there. Had a good supper of pork cutlet, gravy, potatoes, green salad, and Rhine wine (½ liter), all for 2.70 M.

Of all things! Writing this, you acknowledge how unusual it is to stay in a private room in a Hitler Jugend Heim—the home or clubhouse of a Hitler Youth troop. These "homes" were meeting places as well as resting places for youth traveling in the countryside. Your photo shows how absolutely clean and spare this home was.

As a young mathematician on the rise, my father apparently planned in advance to try to meet Konrad Knopp in Tübingen. At this time, he would have no idea of the trail connecting him to Konrad Knopp through others. This is a story told by Sanford L. Segal, professor at the University of Rochester and his future colleague: "Professor Konrad Knopp was the advisor of Werner Meyer-König, who was the advisor of Dieter Gaier, who—years later in the U.S.—had as his advisor John F. Randolph." Dieter Gaier, who would become known for his seminal work in constructive complex analysis, received his Ph.D. from the

University of Rochester in the early fifties. In the acknowledgments for his doctoral dissertation, he wrote: "Professor J.F. Randolph led my way in mathematics and tried always to give me as many experiences as possible." After two years at Harvard University, he returned to Germany and taught at the University of Giessen from 1959 to 1995.

June 11

I bought some rolls, still warm, and took them back to the room. Last night we bought 125 gr. of butter (our first in Germany); it tasted good on the rolls.

On our way to Ebingen we stopped to get a drink and asked a man if it was prettier at Sigmaringen (where we were headed) or Rottweil where we intended to go until the Father at Tübingen advised us the other way. The man said Rottweil and we were about to turn back but decided to ask someone else. The postman and his wife thought the country toward Ebingen prettier but not Ebingen itself. They made out a route for us which we followed and found very beautiful. It went to Strossburgh (*Strassberg*), Frohnstetten, Stetten, Hansen, Beuron, Multheim, and stopped at the youth hostel at Tuttlingen.

Somewhere between Ebingen and Frohnstetten we lost our map and description of this part of Württemberg and the Black Forest. We hope to get another some place but probably will be unable to do so before Freiberg. Stopped at Frohnstetten for more information and a beer. The country around Beuron is very rough and extremely beautiful. We would have 3 mile hills to walk up and then a wonderful ride down.

After getting our beds at the youth hostel we had the grips (which had worked loose) fixed. At supper we attracted a lot of attention and caused considerable amusement to a whole room full of people when we tried to tell the waiters we wanted an egg omelette, potatoes and onions fried together (not the onions in the omelette but the eggs in the omelette and the onions in the potatoes) and lettuce salad.

My one memory of your telling me about this trip is that the two of you biked in the Black Forest. At the time, my adolescent self didn't think to wonder what that was like—whether it was hilly or flat, remote or populated, scenic or boring—and how easy or hard it was using the bicycles of the time.

Jerome K. Jerome, the British humorist writer, provides a glimpse into cycling with friends in the Black Forest in the late 1800s. In *Three Men on the Bummel*,[15] Jerome captures traveling by bicycle in this part of Germany with one (long) sentence:

> We planned a ten-days' tour, which, while completing the Black Forest, should include a spin down the Donau-Thal, which for the twenty miles from Tuttlingen to Sigmaringen is, perhaps, the finest valley in Germany; the Danube stream here winding its narrow way past old-world unspoilt villages; past ancient monasteries, nestling in green pastures, where still the bare-footed and bare-headed friar, his rope girdle tight about his loins, shepherds, with crook in hand, his sheep upon the hill sides; through rocky woods; between sheer walls of cliff, whose every towering crag stands crowned with ruined fortress, church, or castle; together with a blick at the Vosges mountains, where half the population is bitterly pained if you speak to them in French, the

other half being insulted when you address them in German, and the whole indignantly contemptuous at the first sound of English; a state of things that renders conversation with the stranger somewhat nervous work.[16]

This part of your trip requires strength and stamina. I wonder if you trained for your trip by riding bikes when you were in Princeton the previous two years. I don't know how Margaret manages, but you are strong and athletic, as you will be most of your life.

"I took to hard farm labor with gusto," wrote my father later, describing his first summer in Texas when he was 15 years old. A telling description of his continued physical strength and talents appeared in a University of Rochester (U. of R.) newsletter in 1959:

Sports Note: Before a capacity audience the Math Institute defeated the highly rated Science Institute 14–9. It was a tense afternoon as the crowd thrilled to exceptional hitting, fielding, and daringness on the base paths. The man of the afternoon was Dr. Randolph of the University of Rochester Math Department. His terrific speed and tremendous ball handling ability were the highlight of the game. This, however, is nothing new for the diamond ace and as he peddled away on his bicycle I heard him nonchalantly say, "It's all in a day's work."

In 1969, the author of the minute on my father's retirement from the U. of R. at age 65 wrote: "To see him play handball you would suspect him a professional athlete. I used to play with him until I got too old to keep up. He defeats younger men now."

My own memory is riding in the large, metal basket of his bicycle when I was a young child. These days, this would be considered risky, but then it was normal and special at the same time.

June 12

Pretty poor youth hostel. The blankets were heavy as lead. Even so, the five German boys in the small room with me closed all of the windows, pulled the lead coverings over themselves, and went to sleep. I was already asleep before some of the others got in and supposed of course they would open the window. I woke in the middle of the night in a hot sweat. Opened the window. Don't know what the boys thought but they said nothing.

Last night it rained and did not look very clear this morning. We started out and got ready to go to Donaueschingen before a light sprinkle started. Stopped in Donaueschingen and had our big meal at noon and are now (3:05) still sitting here hoping it will clear up so we can go on to Titisee.

Stayed at the hotel where we ate lunch until nearly 5 and it was still raining so we went to the youth hostel. Several other wanderers came at about the same time, but some of them went on later. We talked to a girl from Singen. According to her the hotels in Austria are very good. She also said that the one at Lindau is the best in all the Reich; there is a separate one for "Auslaender" (foreigners). The hostel is run by a Frau. After eating two big bowls apiece of barley soup, good and hot, we felt better. Had quite a talk with some of the boys. Guess the weather had to turn bad so we could see what a wonderful day we had yesterday.

June 13

This morning the sky is still overcast, but we decided to go on anyway. First went back into town to see Donauquelle (*source of the Danube*). There is a cup on a chain there, and we dipped up some water and stuck a finger in it (this seems to be the thing to do). Bought a little belt and a cigar holder.

Three miles or so out of town (at Hansen von Wald (*forest*)) it began to rain harder and was cold and unpleasant, so we decided to have M. go on on the train. She had to wait 40 minutes for the train, which then stopped at every station between there and Titisee. As it happened, I rode up to the Titisee station just as M.'s train was pulling out. Neither of us had to wait a minute for the other.

The heat was on in the station so M. waited there while I looked for a room. Found a beautiful room overlooking the lake with Pension at next house, but when I returned with M. the man would not let us have it. We were soaking wet and undoubtedly looked like the dickens, but it was a dirty trick anyway. Soon found another place in a very nice house; same price and do not have to go out to eat (but we do not have the good view of the lake).

The room is heated and certainly felt good. After washing out some clothes, we climbed into bed and had a good 1½ hour sleep. At supper felt a little self-conscious because the others were much better dressed. Anyway, the food was good and I enjoyed it.

First honest to goodness bath since leaving the Lawrences.

How wonderful to have a bath!

I learn from the Mathematics Department at Cornell University that Vivian Streeter Lawrence and my father were both graduate students and then instructors at Cornell in the early thirties. They both earned their doctorates in mathematics under the same advisor, David Clinton Gillespie.[17] Like many American students of mathematics at the time, Gillespie had studied in Germany. He earned his Ph.D. at Göttingen University under David Hilbert, one of the most influential mathematicians of the twentieth century.

V.S. Lawrence and his wife lived at 1 Lodge Way in Ithaca. It seems that my parents stayed with the Lawrences before going abroad. Since they had just spent two years in Princeton, they would not have had their own place in Ithaca.

June 14

Titisee is 860 m. üM (*über Meer—above sea level*).

Had breakfast in dead silence with the other pensioners about 10. M. went upstairs to wash her pajamas (the only piece of clothing we had that we didn't wash last night), and I went out in search of food and shelter for tonight.

The youth hostel is a fine one, but the beds were already all taken at 11:30 when I was there. However, they sent me to a neighboring house where we have a room for .60 RM apiece. When I paid the bill I found that they had not charged me as much as they had quoted. Guess we looked so bad they felt sorry for us.

Took our things to the new room and went to the youth hostel for lunch. For 35 p apiece had an enormous bowl (at least a liter) of lentils, wieners cut up, and a few potatoes all cooked together. Wasn't bad. Also a slice of bread.

After lunch showed M. chess moves on a board there, and then we went out for a ride. Went along the northern side of the valley for 7 km., mostly up, and then back to Titisee on the other side. Beautiful scenery, and clouds lifted a little.

In Titisee bought rolls, worst, butter, honey, and a bottle of Fechtinger Halde (Elbing) 1934 wine. Made M. feel good. On the way to the room it started to rain again so the wine warmed us up a little (M. a little too much).

To bed early.

June 15

This morning was very cold, but the sun came out at intervals and it looked as if there would be no more rain. We went into town and returned the wine bottle, bought some more rolls, went into a café and bought milk and coffee and sat there eating our own rolls.

The way to Freiberg leads through very beautiful and rough mountainous country. It is called Höllental (*Hell Valley*). The best part of it for us was that it was practically all down hill (14 miles all down).

Got to Freiberg about 11 o'clock, but by the time we were settled in the youth hostel (both in the same room), it was time to eat. After lunch we walked around town. Found the Municipal Theatre and the Rathaus (1557) and of course the "Münster" (*cathedral*). A service was just finishing as we entered.

Had 50 RM changed.

The youth hostel is an old Kloster or Monastery, now owned by the city. The first part of the building was started in 1492. The basement is full of large wine casks where wine is now kept for one large wine house in town.

Charley, an English speaking former "sailor man," is the handy man and told us many interesting things.

June 16

Got up this morning to find it "Sunday" instead of Thursday as we supposed, i.e., it is a big holiday (Corpus Christi day), and everything in town is closed up tight as a drum. Around the Münster and the streets where the priests live behind it were decorated a great deal. Many very nice statues of Christ, Mary, and other holy figures were placed out on window sills, in doorways, or in specially built altars and surrounded by many flowers and green plants and candles. Most of them were very beautiful. The streets were crowded with people.

Christian procession in Freiberg

A procession was to start at 10:30, but we had about decided not to stay. However, the procession formed on the street we should take toward Triberg, so when we got to the front of the procession we stopped. The procession started soon afterward, everyone walking.

There were many banners, Biblical figures mounted on frameworks and carried on shoulders, and people in costumes. The Archbishop was surrounded by other high officials and walked under a very large canopy and carried a large silver candlestick-looking affair. We understand that, because of the present government, the procession is not as long and not nearly as colorful as in former years.

During the procession we heard someone talking English behind us. It turned out to be an English woman, her aunt (a German), and nephew (a 19-year-old soldier of the German army). After the procession was over we all went up to the aunt's house and had some liqueur and cookies, both very good.

Did not get started on our way until nearly 10 o'clock. It is around 60 km. to Triberg, but we got there at 6:30. Went to Waldkirch, Elzach, Oberprechtal, Triberg. From Ob. Prechtal we had to walk about an hour the way was so steep up. We then had a good coast down to Triberg.

The youth hostel was full, but there is a second youth hostel where we got beds, so called.

When I was growing up, I loved to flip through the pages of Time and Life Magazines, which were piled on the end tables in our living room. I've been thinking that you and Margaret probably read these magazines in the months before your trip. Reading the issues from 1937 and early 1938, I learn about the Europe you are visiting and the events as seen from this side of the Atlantic.

Throughout the thirties, the American press generally held back from reporting or focusing on persecution of the Jews and instead reported on other events in Germany such as elections and boycotts. Before Kristallnacht in November 1938, there was a widespread sense of skepticism and confusion about the accuracy of any reports of antisemitic violence or persecution and a failure of will to pursue them. Tragically, this affected both American governmental policy as well as what

Americans felt and knew about was going on in Germany.[18] However, *Time* Magazine did cover Nazi activities and made its opinions known.

I find the writing in *Time* Magazine fascinating with its frank fear and loathing of Nazism and its bold, often ironic, use of language. For example, my parents may have read this in the December 27, 1937 issue:

> All Christian churches in Germany have taken such a beating from the Nazi regime in 1937 that good Nazi adherents had begun to wonder whether it would be politically safe this year for them to celebrate Christmas. Taking up this vital question, Das Schwarze Korps, organ of Adolf Hitler's black-uniformed Special Guard, which consistently baits Jews, Catholics, Protestants, last week assured Germans that they might observe Christmas without being guilty of "un-German practices." It asserted: "Christmas is no intellectual property of the Christian confessions. They simply borrowed it without asking permission . . . This holiday is the exclusive property of Germans!"

Growing up in a non-church-going household, naturally I became interested in religion. My father was an agnostic, but he drove me to Third Presbyterian Church because I asked him to. My path took me from a short period of fervent listening as a pre-teen to Billy Graham on the radio to an academic interest in Eastern religions to a happy landing in Quakerism and Sufism.

In the year before my father died, he came with me to the Quaker meeting for worship in Rochester. He liked it—the silence, the messages about life and light—and he mentioned that he preferred this kind of service for a memorial rather than a traditional church service. We did this for him.

June 17

M. looked at wood carvings while I attended to cashing some money and sending a letter. We bought a cute owl clothes brush holder.

The road out of Triberg was up and up, then down and down, etc. Went to St. Georgen, Schramberg, and Freudenstadt. Just before Schramberg we stopped at a sort of country store to get some milk for lunch, 1 liter for 30 p. They then let us go into their regular dining room to eat our lunch. They are all for Hitler and enjoyed telling us how much better everything is now than before he came. I bought a polished cow horn used by the natives to hang on their belts to hold files to sharpen their scythes.

Got to Freudenstadt about 7. At the Gasthaus König Karl the proprietor would not let us sit in the end of the restaurant where the tables had cloths. He later gave quite a discourse to a table full of Germans. He talked in a loud voice (evidently for our benefit) and although we understood little of what he said, it was certainly derogatory to the English.

One traveler in the 1938 Hand-Me-Down Guide describes Freudenstadt as a "charming resort town." Unfortunately, you two English-speaking travelers are evidently linked (or confused) in the mind of the proprietor with the British and are ostracized from the higher end section of the restaurant. Perhaps you are too scruffy looking. Also, this isn't the first time you two are rejected or turned aside as you try to find lodging or meals. It has occurred to me that Margaret may look "Jewish." At a time of heightened sensitivity to Jewish identity, her dark appearance may be creating

problems for you. In any case, if you are keeping up with current events, you know that the British are unpopular in Germany.

In May, just before my parents arrived in Europe, the British under Prime Minister Neville Chamberlain and Lord Halifax successfully averted a crisis when they warned Hitler off invading Czechoslovakia—or so people thought. In German eyes, the British were getting in the way of their Führer's plans.

I can tell you don't like the attitude of the proprietor, whether you identify with the British or not. It is your nature to be independent and to think for yourself. You wouldn't like a scene where someone is trying to persuade others of a certain viewpoint based on national identity.

But what do you think when the people in the country store tell you life is better under Hitler? At this time the majority of Germans believe that Hitler is bringing good times to the country with an economic turnaround.[19] And for many Germans, the country feels safer, more decent, and more moral as well as stronger and more unified.[20]

In your papers I find a letter from a German engineer you meet on this trip, dated December 1938: "One hears different things concerning America, papers and pamphlets spread all over the German Reich. You realize don't you that in Germany there is not a single unemployed, and no man that goes hungry in winter or freezes, and this is not so of any other country except Italy which is also under state's direction. In Germany order and discipline rule. You were here yourself and saw it." I don't know what you think about this.

June 18

My bed had a mountain range down the middle, but I managed to get a fairly good sleep. Had some of their malz (*malt*) coffee this morning that was not bad. The sky is nearly cloudless, and this is the warmest day we have had for some time.

Here the farmers seem more prosperous than between Freiberg and Triberg, but the houses are not nearly so picturesque.

We were told that the way was nearly all down hill to Baden-Baden, and it probably would have been if we had gone a different way, but we chose to go by the Mummelsee (*a deep lake surrounded by forest*). Practically all morning we walked pushing the bikes. At Mummelsee we had beer and rolls and were surprised at how little they cost.

The mountains are very rugged here and the way was very beautiful, if hard. Mummelsee itself is 1036 m. above sea level. The highest point in the Northern Black Forest (Hornisgrinde 1164 m.) is very close, but we did not have the energy to climb it. Anyway the atmosphere was not clear because of the heat quivers.

After leaving Mummelsee we expected to go down, but were fooled again. We had to climb some little distance yet (after a short tantalizing coast). However, the road did turn down eventually and we had a wonderful ride down. If we could have only straightened the road out and made it less steep we surely could have coasted clear to Heidelberg.

Got to Baden-Baden about 6 and found the youth hostel. It is the first floor and basement of a school house, the upper floors of which are still used for school.

Had supper and then took a ride along the Lichtenthaler Allee. This "Allee" is really a long narrow park with most beautiful trees. Many of the big expensive hotels (and there are many of them) are near the Allee.

Your day sounds so enjoyable and the setting so beautiful. How could you possibly know that five months later, the town of Baden-Baden, where you end your day of cycling, will burst into flames? In the early morning of November 10, 1938, the town's Jews will be rounded up and humiliated in the streets, and later that day the synagogue in Baden-Baden will be burned to the ground during what later will become known as Kristallnacht (Night of Glass or Crystal Night) or Pogromnacht. [21] *Local people will break the windows of Jewish shops and homes and destroy furniture and belongings in the city, as they will in towns and cities throughout Germany.*

During a rampage that was actually a coordinated attack by the Nazi government, more than 1,000 synagogues in Germany were burned or destroyed. This followed the shooting of German embassy official Ernst Vom Rath in Paris by seventeen-year-old Herschel Grynszpan, a Polish Jewish student—providing the spark for an opportunity for the Nazis to retaliate. Kristallnacht meant that Jews could no longer assume the current regime would soon be over. November 9-10 is marked as the official beginning of the Holocaust.

In her novel, *Stones from the River,* Ursula Hegi writes about Kristallnacht in the town of Burgdorf:

> For weeks, the smoke hung above the town, getting into your lungs with each breath, making you cough; and after the rubble was cleaned up, you would still come across slivers of glass far from the areas of destruction as if they'd been carried there by the smoke. You wouldn't see them unless you'd step into one of them, say, or catch the reflection of a shard of sun in a bare tree limb while reaching up

to hang out your laundry in the frosty winter air, making you feel as if you and your neighborhood, the world even, were held in the eye of a splintered mirror.[22]

June 19

There was an organized party of about 20 little boys (8–12) in my room and about the same size party of girls in M.'s room. Consequently, we were awakened early. Had breakfast over and were in town a little after 8 o'clock. Drank some of their hot salt water; there are fountains right on the street. The water is supposed to be good for rheumatoid arthritis and gout.[23] The people all carry little flattened glasses and stand around the fountain each drinking his prescribed number of glasses.

Went in the building where two springs owned by the Friedrichsbad are. The water comes from 2,000 m. underground at a temperature varying from 130 degrees to 150 degrees f. Also visited the ruins of the Roman baths.

Left town close to 11 o'clock. A little out of town stopped for 30 minutes or so to watch an airplane pull a glider into the air. The glider roared over us for some time as we went on our way.

The road was slightly down hill and the wind was to the side and a little in our favor so we made good time. About 1 o'clock I had a puncture in my rear tire. Luckily we were only 100 yards or so from a road side place. Two fellows there had patching and worked on the tire for me. They could not agree on the proper way to do anything, but eventually they got the tire off, patched, and on again. It has held ever since.

Got to Bruchsal about 5 and decided to stop. We are both tired and the next youth hostel is some 10 or 12 miles further on. Anyway it is only 18 or 20 miles to Heidelberg. Rather poor supper and to bed early.

In 1937, the Nazis forbade Jews to use the mineral baths in Baden-Baden. I wonder if you know this. The Jews who are rounded up in Baden-Baden on November 10 will be deported to Dachau.

Kristallnacht will also descend on Bruchsal. Local people will break all the shop windows of Jewish businesses in the city and burn down the synagogue.[24] On June 19, as you ride your bikes into Bruchsal and look for the youth hostel, you cannot imagine this, I am sure.

Two years later, in October 1940, the last remaining Jews in Baden-Baden and Bruchsal were deported to the Gurs concentration camp in southwest France.[25] In March 1943, those Jews remaining in the Vichy camps, mainly Gurs, were deported to Auschwitz.[26]

During the war, Bruchsal housed a detention center, described in a biography of Noor-unnisa Inayat Khan, the daughter of Inayat Khan, who brought Sufism to the West from India in the 1920s. Sufism is sometimes called "the path of the heart," a spiritual path where one seeks the divine presence in all life. The Sufi message expresses awareness of the essential unity of all world religions.

Noor was a sensitive young woman who wrote poetry but had found within herself a deep calling to resist the Nazis. She became a radio operator working for the Resistance in Paris under the code name of "Madeleine." In 1943, she was captured and imprisoned at the Paris headquarters of the Germans along with a British officer and a French Colonel, Leon Faye.

Eventually, Colonel Faye was moved to Bruchsal, where he was kept "with hands and feet in chains." After the war, his notes were found "behind the radiator in the cell he had occupied at Bruchsal, folded into an infinite number of small pleats, to escape detection by the guards."[27] Noor was sent to Dachau where she was tortured and killed.

In 2004, Farid and I visited the home where Noor grew up, in Suresnes, outside of Paris. We wanted to visit the home of Inayat Khan because of our connection to Sufism. From our hotel in Paris we took the Metro to the end of line 1 at Porte Maillot and then a bus, which wound through the Bois de Boulogne to Suresnes, now a suburb. In the twenties and thirties, Suresnes was still in the country, and the house was surrounded by gardens and open meadows.

The wall in front of the spacious stone house known as Fazal Manzil contains a plaque that reads in French: "Here lived Noor Inayat Khan 1914–44, Called Madeleine in the Resistance, Shot at Dachau, Radio operator for the Buckmaster network, Awarded the French Croix de Guerre 1939–1945 and the George Cross." Looking at the plaque, we felt the intersection of our deep interests in Sufism, nonviolence, and the amazing ability of some to speak truth to power.

June 20

Were lazy this morning and did not get away until nearly 9:30. Went by the large castle and looked at the buildings (but did not go in) and walked through the garden (which would be very pretty if it were not for the statues).[28]

Got to Heidelberg about 11:30 and went to Pension Elite.[29] Had the proprietor take a picture of us with the bikes.

Got my shirt at laundry and returned bicycles and got refund. M. walked back to Pension and I walked out to the youth hostel, got bags, and took train back to Pension. Had lunch at P. In the afternoon we washed up a few things and took a walk.

Tried to find a movie in English but find that there are none in town and probably none in Germany. This is funny because a good many of the films are American. After supper we were both very tired and went to bed very early.

In front of the Pension Elite in Heidelberg

Now I see that you left your bags at the youth hostel in Heidelberg, back on June 6. This freed you to go on your cycling trip.

In the photograph in front of the Pension Elite, Margaret stands next to her bicycle, her hands resting on the wool blankets in the bike rack, several feet away from you, her husband. She smiles gently. Even though you do not stand close to one another, perhaps because of the bicycles, you both appear relaxed and happy.

In your knickers and short-sleeved shirt, you look vigorous and tanned, your arms sinewy muscled and strong. Your bicycle holds the larger bag, tied up with rope. You are a good rope tier. You found this skill handy as a young ranch hand in Texas, and later on you will entertain my brother and me with rope tricks you learned from your father.

About trying to find a movie in English...after 1933, film became another area of cultural control under the direction of Hitler's propaganda minister, Joseph Goebbels. One goal was to increase domestic production of films and decrease the importing of foreign films; American films were still shown in 1938 but were banned later after the war began.[30]

June 21

Got up just in time to catch the train at 10:01 for Nürnberg (*Nuremberg*). Ate a little breakfast on the train. Talked to a German on the train who had spent several years in America on Wall St.

At Nürnberg checked our bags and took knapsack to the youth hostel. There are several youth hostels in N. but none for both men and women. M. is at least five blocks from me.

Took the first roll of film to Photo Post, Lorenzplatz 15, to be developed. Had a scare because the clerk opened the light proof cartridge under a light. However, an hour later the development of the roll showed no ill effects.

Had a dish of wurst and ½ l. beer at the Bratwurstglocklein erected in 1313. A little tiny place but world famous.[31] Walked around a bit and bought some Lebkuchen (life cake, a kind of gingerbread) for which Nürnberg is also famous.

Noticed that at the opera this is a "Festspielwoche" (*festival week*) and that on Thursday night "Die Meistersinger von Nürnberg" (*The Mastersingers of Nuremburg*) will be given. Inquired prices and were surprised that we could get fairly good tickets for 3.00 RM apiece (i.e., 75 cents). Altered our plans to remain an extra day and bought the tickets.

As usual, I'm curious. Did you ask the German who had lived in the States about what is going on in Germany? I want to know what you talked about!

And do you know that Nuremberg is where huge Nazi Party rallies have been taking place since Hitler came to power in

1933? In the past five years, these rallies have become settings for explosive antisemitic speeches and Nazi propaganda.

At the 1935 rally, Hitler announced the passage of the "Nuremberg Laws," which formalized the antisemitic measures taken in the previous years. Beginning with the words, "Entirely convinced that the purity of German blood is essential to the further existence of the German people," the first set of laws to protect "German blood and German honor" prohibited marriage between "Germans" and Jews" among other things. The Reich Citizenship Law stripped individuals who were not considered German of their rights as German citizens. After the war, Nuremberg will be the setting for the trials of many of those German citizens of the Reich for their Holocaust crimes.

June 22

Met M. at her youth hostel at 8:30 and had breakfast. Then went to see first the church (*St. Katherine's*), which is the scene of the first act of Die Meistersinger.[32] Then went around to the Hans Sachs (shoemaker-poet-mastersinger featured in the opera) house where the workshop is restored supposedly as Sachs had it. However, some additions to the house have been made so it does not look exactly as it does in the opera. Had wine and Lebkuchen in the shop there. Did not go to the place along the river where the third act is supposed to have taken place.

Had lunch in the Nassauer Keller, very interesting, good food and not very expensive.[33] In the afternoon bought an etching of Dürer's and also an English libretto of Die Meistersinger.

At noon watched the clock perform.[34] At night watched people go in the opera.

You and Margaret learn about Richard Wagner's opera, Die Meistersinger von Nürnberg, the way you both approached a new interest—by reading, research, and personal experience—all the ways you passed on to me and that I use now to find out about your trip. I see that you are delighted by the music and humor of this opera, performed right in Nuremberg.

In 2007, I happened to notice that Die Meistersinger was being performed at the Metropolitan Opera in New York City. For a few minutes I was excited to think that I might be able to see it at the Met. I looked on the website for information about tickets and found that for one thing, it was sold out for the last remaining performance that I could attend, and for another, ticket prices were no longer anywhere near the 75 cents my parents paid in 1938. Today, at the Met, one could spend up to $375 to see this opera. I gave up trying but will be on the lookout for a future performance (or buy the DVD).

As a comic opera, this work was a departure for Wagner, the composer of Romantic music and drama, who felt that his work could unify Germany culturally and politically. The Nazis promoted Wagner's music because it was purely German, being sung in German and based on Germanic legends, although Wagner did not specifically express antisemitism in his operas. However, Wagner's apocalyptic and "redemptive anti-Semitism," a world view that saw redemption coming from freedom from the Jews in German society, has been discussed by historian Saul Friedlander.[35]

In "The Myth of the German Soul," an essay published in *Das Neue Tage-Buch* on March 12, 1938, German journalist Joseph Roth wrote, "There's no doubt that a lot of the world's indifference toward the terrible things going on in Germany has to do with the European Wagner fixation." He said that Europeans are smitten by the myth of the irrational German soul and view current events through the romantic lens of German theater and opera. "This way of viewing the German scene is not new to the present rulers of Germany, and they know exactly how best to exploit it: both in their internal dealings with their population, and—more dangerous still—externally. . . . The machine spirit, the Prussian drill, has shrouded itself in German mythology. And what we call 'the European world' has 'bought it.'"

I would love to try seeing this opera through your eyes. Do you also look at current events through the romantic lens of German opera? I like to think not but perhaps partly you do.

June 23

Last night the whole 25 Germans sleeping in my room got up at 3 o'clock to hear the Schmeling-Louis fight. The radio was going so loudly in a neighboring room that I also got up, but before I got there the fight was over.[36]

This morning we looked up a Pension and moved ourselves and bag in. M. had her hair washed. In the afternoon walked around a little, bought Lebkuchen, got caught in a shower, read Die Meistersinger and slept. Tonight went to the opera.

The opera was wonderful (even if the prince did have a beer belly and weighed at least 250 lbs.).[37]

I certainly approve of the Germans' way of eating (if I don't approve of what they eat). In intermission many took out rolls, slices of ham or wurst, cakes or what not, got a bottle of beer and set to for a dainty repast.

Looking down on the lobby you could count the men in dress clothes on one hand and not over half of the women were dressed. No one in our (third) balcony was dressed. One fellow came in shorts.

This is different! I can't imagine Americans having a picnic at the opera—unless it's summer and they're on the grass at Tanglewood in the Berkshires or Highland Park in Rochester, NY, where as a teenager I thrilled to the romance of Bizet's Carmen. What you like about the picnic is the Germans' ingenuity and thriftiness.

Of course, the audience is completely non-Jewish. By this time, Jews are not welcome in audiences; in 1933, they were banned by Goebbels from employment in culture, music, art, film, and theater. Moreover, performances of Wagner and other artists of "German" origin are not even permitted for the Jewish Cultural Association, the one venue that provided entertainment and employment for Jews in the arts.[38] I have no idea if my parents know any of this.

You don't write about the fight, but I'm not surprised. The only organized sport you follow is tennis, and you prefer playing to watching (the same is true of softball). But I am curious... how did the young Germans in the youth hostel take it? Were they crushed? Angry? Scared? Although I never knew you to be particularly patriotic—and I'm pretty sure you didn't like boxing—I hope you were glad that Americans, black and white, came together to celebrate a symbolic victory over the Nazis.

The boxing match on the evening of June 22, 1938, between Max Schmeling, portrayed by the Nazis as a symbol of Aryan supremacy, and Joe Louis, representing democracy and America (even though racial equality was not in sight), was much more than just a boxing match. Later it became known as "the fight of the century."

Two years earlier, Jesse Owens, the black American sprinter, won four gold medals at the 1936 Olympics in Munich. This infuriated Hitler. But two months before that fight, Joe

Louis had lost to Schmeling. Now Louis wanted revenge and to win back the honor and respect of black America.

With Yankee Stadium filled, and millions listening to the radio in the U.S. and around the world, Louis knocked out Schmeling in two minutes and four seconds. Joe Louis would become the greatest heavyweight champion in history. Schmeling, who was used by the Nazis, actually opposed them: he refused to join the Nazi party, and he hid two Jewish boys in his Berlin apartment during Kristallnacht.

June 24

I took the knapsack and two suitcases to the station because M. had to go to the youth hostel to get her "Ausweis" (*youth hostel pass*) that we forgot to get yesterday morning when we left.

Had to change trains twice before getting to Rothenburg. Then we checked our bags and started out with the knapsack in search of the youth hostel. Some directed us to a youth hostel and others said there was none now; the latter turned out to be correct. Decided to see as much as possible and go on to Munich.

Rothenburg is a very picturesque little town practically all still within its ancient walls. Saw the drinking ceremony at the Rathaus at 12.[39] Walked nearly all over town and went up in the highest tower of the wall, located at the old main gate. On the way down we decided to walk for a little distance on the wall and then go down to the station to catch our train. We began to think (after about 1/4 of a mile) that we would have to go back in order to get down (and then we would miss our train). However we called down the 20 ft. or so to a man who told us go ahead to the second tower. We got down there all right.

Arrived in Munich about 5 and I started out to find the youth hostel. M. and I got on a tram with all of our bags and rode 15 or 20 minutes and then I left M. with the bags and went to the youth hostel and got beds. Back to M., decided to get room, cancelled youth hostel, back to Bahnhof (*train station*), left M. with bags, found room, went back for M. and finally got located in the room. Dead tired.

German citizens were required to carry an Ausweis or identity card, which they would need to show authorities at any time. As part of the increased persecution of Jews in the summer of 1938, the Nazis would promulgate a new law on August 17 (to be effective January 1, 1939) making it mandatory for Jews to add the name Israel or Sara to their existing names and identity cards. This would mean that Jews could be automatically and quickly identified as Jewish.[40]

My mother's Ausweis was her youth hostel permit, issued by the Association of German Youth Hostels, which included space for each youth hostel's stamp and dates of stay at the hostel.

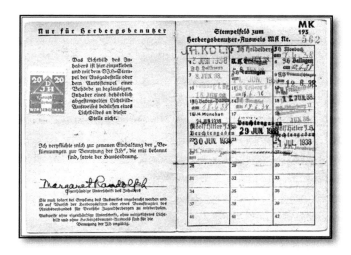

With its narrow, winding streets and high walls, Rothenburg ob der Tauber (above the Tauber River) is a main stop along the northern Romantic Road. It is surrounded by a town wall of 3.5 kilometers.

You are so responsible! How tiring that must be . . . and how boring for Margaret. Do you ever stay with the bags while she goes out to look for a room? I don't ask this in an accusing tone (it sounds it), but from real curiosity. Is it a matter of personality or a custom of the time?

June 25

Got up rather late and looked a little for another room because ours is noisy, but decided to spend no more time. Walked around locating things and ourselves. Ate dinner at one of the many large eating places along Neuhauserstrasse. This P.M. also walked to many places of interest; down Maximilianstrasse. To the Isar river, along the river to Prinz Regentenstrasse into the English Gardens (beer at the Chinese tower) and then to the University (*University of Munich aka Ludwig-Maximilians Universität*). Looked at math books but found none I wanted. Got Carathéodory's address (Rauchstrasse 8/2).[41]

Went to the Hofbräu Haus where each of us got a liter of beer.[42] A German fellow came in who had been in America 14 months. We enjoyed talking to him very much and have made arrangements to meet him again Monday night at 7:30. Got to bed about 12.

June 26

Started out to go to "Alte Pinakothek"[43] (*"Old Art Gallery"*) but I stopped to photograph the Protestant church being torn down to make a parking place for the "Day of German Art" July 8–10. Met M. at A.P. and was surprised at how much I enjoyed looking at the pictures.

Church being razed in preparation for Day of German Art

Lunch at the "Löwenbräu-München"[44] and then to the Deutsches Museum.[45] Made a list of the things we wanted to see and saw them all and some more also. Were there four hours and hated to leave. Everything is so realistic and so many things can be "worked," e.g., running in a real treadmill.

On the way home saw a fellow with a really marvelous costume and asked him if we could take his picture, he was tickled to death. He had a long pipe and promised to go with me tomorrow so I can buy one.

The "Day of German Art," consisted of art exhibits celebrating the superiority of German art in contrast to modern "degenerate art." Parades went through Munich under the banner, "2000 Years of German Culture." The Germans must have acted quickly in tearing down the church since it was only a couple of weeks before the "celebration." This reminds me of my mother's clipping about Karl Hofer, who was considered modern and degenerate.

You love tinkering with things, making them work if they don't, making them work better, putting them back together if they are falling apart, like the "tennis" rackets you will make out of old squash rackets for your grandchildren.

June 27

Karl (of the costume) was true to his word and took me to a little place where they make many of the wooden pipes you see in the stores. Everything seemed very reasonable, so I brought M. back and we bought other things also. M. took a picture of Karl and me (and the pipes).

In the afternoon M. looked at Salzburg sweaters, dirndles, etc. (but bought nothing) and I went to Carathéodory's home. Had a nice chat with him, Mrs. C. and their son.

Had supper at Hofbräu Häus (so we could take some pictures). The fellow we met night before last came in with bread and cheese. Took his picture also. After supper he went with us to several places of interest we had not seen yet, among them Königsplatz, where the bodies of the 12 men who fell November 9, 1923, the first to die for the National-Socialist movement were buried.[46] Later he took us by train to Schwabing (the Bohemia of Munich) and had wine in one of the artists' wine stube (*cozy restaurant serving wine, perhaps run by an artist*) there. Got home about 11:30.

Lottery for jobs in Munich

A Hitler look-alike running the lottery

In 1938, it seems harmless to smoke a pipe. I'm sure you are very excited about buying a pipe in Germany.

Growing up, I associated pipes with my father and liked them. They had a tangy, slightly sweet yet masculine smell that permanently came to rest inside his tweed jackets. He had a routine of knocking them and cleaning them with pipe cleaners, which were fun to twist into crazy shapes.

You must be thrilled to meet Constantin Carathéodory since the subject of your doctoral dissertation was "Carathéodory Measure and a Generalization of the Gauss-Green Lemma" (Cornell University, 1934).

Mathematician Constantin Carathéodory

Carathéodory was one of the "most internationally famous mathematicians of the time. …[he was] a Greek national (though a German citizen) who essentially removed himself from political involvement during the Nazi years."[47] Sanford L. Segal notes several instances of Carathéodory helping colleagues through difficulties such as writing letters of support. I would love to know whether he spoke to my father about life as a mathematician under Nazi rule.

As a member at the Institute for Advanced Study in Princeton, New Jersey, for the two years immediately before this trip, my father spent some of his time on measure theory. I was glad to discover in a box of his papers some reprints of his journal articles from the Institute: an article coauthored with Anthony P. Morse on "Gillespie Measure" appeared in the *Duke Mathematics Journal* in 1940 and was reprinted in 1945 in *Fundamenta Mathematicae*.[48] Another was "The Vitali Covering Theorem for Carathéodory Linear Measure," published in *The Annals of Mathematics* in 1939.[49]

In later years, my father wrote college mathematics textbooks. The first—*Calculus and Analytic Geometry*—was coauthored with Mark Kac, his colleague at Cornell in the late thirties and early forties. After earning his doctorate in mathematics in 1937, Kac, who was a Polish Jew, decided to leave Poland as soon as he could. He left by ship in late November 1938.

In his autobiography, he wrote, "The political situation was grave—it had been two months since Munich—but we did not dream of what lay ahead." He and his family were full of hope that he could arrange to stay in the United States permanently and ultimately send for his parents and brother. At that time, "I don't think that anyone dreamed of the horror that was to come." But it did come.

"In less than a year the world exploded and much of my part of it was consumed by flames. Millions, including my parents and my brother, were murdered by the Germans, and many disappeared without a trace in the vastness of the Soviet Union."[50]

Mark Kac earned a scholarship to go to Johns Hopkins in 1938; a year later Cornell offered him a position as an instructor in 1939. In 1951, he spent his sabbatical year at the Institute for Advanced Study.

I can only guess that my father and his colleague must have talked about this trip in 1938 and the circumstances under which Kac left Europe.

June 28

The air raid practice was not very interesting. We hung around the Rathaus waiting for it from 10 to 11:30. Only went into a regular wine cellar. A fellow taking pictures was taken with his camera by the officers.

Went to Löwenbräu-München for lunch and afterward saw the brewery— 500,000 liters per day. Met some Americans (not very interesting) from Ohio.

Ate in room but went out for beer later.

About the air raid practice and picture taking: most likely, there were sirens, and then you had to take shelter in the wine cellar. The officers (might they be the local SS?) may have suspected the man taking pictures of being a spy, or they might forbid picture taking within public buildings, especially during an air raid practice (in preparation for the future reality). This is one of those situations where you as travelers witness an action but do not know the reason or social context for it. If you ask someone, will you get in trouble? Or does your instinct tell you to observe and not ask questions?

June 29

Wednesday. This has been one hectic day. Our train left Munich this morning at 8:55 and we did not get up until 8. When we had only 10 minutes, M. still did not have her dress on, and I was closing my bags. I took the bags and went on as M. could run with the knapsack and coats. We made the train, but that is about all.

On the way to Prien there was a freight train wreck that held us up for some time.

Took the little dinky train to Chiemsee and then the boat for the island on which the Ludwig castle Herrenchiemsee[51] is located. A very nice little boat ride with high mountains rising to the south (our right) and flat fertile country to the north. Had lunch of cheese, bread, and beer in the hotel garden and were surprised that it cost so little. 15 minute walk to the castle.

The castle surpasses any of my wildest visions of what it would be like. The marble is so white, the paintings (especially those on the ceilings) so beautiful, and the carved gold plated bronze so intricate and so much of it that it is really unbelievable. Enormous mirrors absolutely flawless and hundreds of them. The king's dressing room (off the bath, which is really a swimming pool) took 30 people 7 years to build. The draperies of the castle, all hand made, took 300 people 7 years to make. Each chandelier (and there are many in each room) is very elaborate carved bronze (gold plated) or glass and holds at least 50 candles. Twice a year now all of the candles are lit; it must be quite a sight.

After going through the castle went back to Prien. When the train came in M. went to the front and I to the back to find seats. I found none so got off with the bags just as the conductor signaled the train to start. All the doors were closed so I dropped my bag, opened a door of the moving train, threw M.'s bag in, ran back for my bag, opened another door and threw my bag in and then jumped on the train myself. Dangerous, but I go there. Took my bag and walked forward to the next car where M.'s bag was and took the two bags on forward to the car where M. was. Her car was crowded so we took the back pack and went back to a less crowded car. The next stop I got off, ran forward, and brought M.'s bag back before the train started. The next stop I got off to get my bag only to find that the train had divided and the car with my bag had gone on to Salzburg and from there might go on to almost anywhere in Austria or Italy.

As soon as we arrived in Berchtesgaden we reported the loss and had a time doing so as no one spoke English well. They had me fill out a blank and they telephoned and told me to come back later.

I went to the youth hostel (while M. sat on her bag) and got beds. Ate supper and went back to station.

They said the bag was located in Salzburg and would be in on the 7:40 train. We met the train, but no bag. Telephoned to Salzburg and they said the bag would be sent on the 21:23 train. This was too late to get in youth hostel so we left instructions to put bag in baggage room.

The clouds are so low that we cannot see the mountains, but only enough to see that they must be high and rugged.

So to bed.

You are living on the edge this day. I want to know how both of you handle it. Is Margaret angry at you? Does she blame you for getting off the train in the first place? And then for getting off at various stops to retrieve the bags? On the surface, that seems like a creative solution to crowded conditions, but risky . . . and stubborn. You could be stubborn. And how do you feel? As a man, and a man of your times, you may feel like a failure. It is important to you to be organized, orderly, and prepared. Do you feel that you let her down?

In these pages, you don't write about your marriage or how you are getting along during this long trip abroad. I assume that you enjoy being together, riding bikes, having picnics, drinking beer, and talking to people you meet along the way. I can't help but notice (and appreciate) how well you seem to travel together.

When I lose a bag on a trip, I temporarily lose my bearings. It's hard to go on without those items that mean comfort and familiarity—the little blue comb, the soft washcloth, the novel I started reading at home. And what was in your bag?

June 30

Thursday. At the station they said "Die bag has not been founded." More telephone calls; more filling out of blanks; more everything but no word of bag. These fellows will do absolutely nothing on their own initiative. We must ask "Could some of the cars have gone to Wien?" (*Vienna*) "Yes, perhaps." "Can you telephone Wien?" "Yes." "Will you telephone Wien?" "Yes, tomorrow." Can you telephone today?" "Yes." "Will you telephone now?" "Yes." Telephones to Wien. "Could a car from this train have gone to Villoc (*Villach, in southern Austria*)? "Yes." Etc., etc. for München.

In afternoon went to Königsee (*King Lake*) and rowed around for an hour in a flat bottomed boat. Beautiful scenery but we did not enjoy it.

Back in Berchtesgaden met the same train we came in on yesterday and told the conductor all of what had happened. He telephoned Salzburg and they have the bag and are sending it on the 7:40. We met the 7:40 and (as last night) no bag. Telephoned Salzburg and they say a woman has claimed the bag and gone off with it.

Finally they agree to telephone every station in Austria. At Klagenfurt (*in southern Austria*) they have a bag that seems to fit the description, but it is late and the bag is locked in a room that the man cannot get to. "In the morning you come back and we will send a telegram telling the man at Klagenfurt to send the bag." (Why he didn't tell him to send it while talking with him I do not know.) "Yes, I will come back early.

How early will you be here so we can telegraph?" "I come to work at 5 o'clock." "Could we send the telegram tonight?" "Yes." "Will you telegraph tonight" etc., etc. Finally, he sends the telegram tonight.

The clouds lifted today so we could see the peaks. They are so much higher and more rugged than we expected, and a great deal of snow on them.

The first train from Klagenfurt comes at 13:53 so we must wait until afternoon tomorrow before leaving.

As the train pulled apart on June 29, it tore the fabric of your journey. One moment the bag is there, with you; the next moment it's hurtling off in another direction. "Wait!" you cry, arm outstretched, "come back."

No longer are you engrossed in your trip. Now the most important thing in your life is to find the bag, and you change your plans accordingly. Now, you sound more worried. It occurs to me that already, all around you, Jews are losing their possessions. Little by little, they are losing their civil rights, their freedom to move around, and their livelihoods. In only four months, after Kristallnacht on November 9, thousands of Jews will lose everything. In that light, your observation, "These fellows will do absolutely nothing on their own initiative" chills me.

July 1

Friday. This morning the station man says he had talked with Klagenfurt and it surely is the bag. However, instead of coming on the 13:53 train it will not arrive until 19:40. There is nothing to do then but to wait.

We went to the Reiseburo (travel agency) to see about getting our Austrian tickets. Figured how we could save $2.40 but another fellow came in and said we couldn't do it.

Had lunch and then M. went to Salzburg. I went for a walk up toward the Führer's house. There are a great many workmen all over the mountain making all kinds of roads that I see no ordinary use for. It is really astounding the number of men there are at work. I could not go the Führer's house but of course did not think I could do so.

Walked on around the mountain on a very nice path and got an excellent view of Watzmann (2713 m.) (*Mt. Watzmann, a peak of the Salzburg Alps*), Königsee and the mountains around it.

Allowed myself two hours to get back, eat supper, and meet the 19:40 and my bag. However, the bag was not on the train. I thought surely it would be this time. They called Salzburg but could find no trace of the bag. Could not hear Klagenfurt very well but think they said bag had been sent. Stayed for the next two trains from Salzburg but the bag was not on either.

Got a telephone call through to the Jugendherberge in Salzburg, but M. was not in probably because she was meeting the train I would have gone on.

At 10:30 started up to the youth hostel in hopes of getting a room. An Austrian fellow also tried to get in, but all doors were locked and we could arouse no one. After a while I started back to Berchtesgaden. However, it was so late that when I passed a field with freshly cut and piled hay, I went in and fixed a bed.

You call him the Führer, as is the custom among Germans and Austrians. The use of a title, instead of a name, confers authority on a person. It reminds me of bureaucrats who refer to "the deputy commissioner," assuming that I will know who the person is, or if I don't, it doesn't matter because he or she has the author-

ity to make the final decision. We Americans normally call our president by his name, but sometimes we say "the President." It seems that you (and those around you) avoid naming the person—Adolph Hitler—and accept instead his identity as Leader.

I notice that you are curious to see Hitler's house (the Berghof). Are you looking for anything in particular? That an amazing number of men are making roads you see no ordinary use for has a sinister ring now. You are right. Whatever Hitler did, there was "no ordinary use for." Little do you know that you are witnessing the construction of Hitler's Kehlsteinhaus, the "Eagle's Nest," far above the Berghof.

The chalets of Adolf Hitler, Hermann Göring, Martin Bormann, and other Nazi leaders, with air-raid shelters, barracks, and various installations (all destroyed in an Allied air attack in April 1945) had been built on the Obersalzberg, 500 meters above the town of Berchtesgaden.

However, the workmen were working on the "Eagle's Nest," a retreat even farther up the neighboring Kehlstein mountain. This enormous project required thousands of workers blasting a road into the mountain. To access the main building, they built a tunnel into the mountain, followed by an elevator. In the summer of 1938, work on the site was frantic and took place day and night.

Will you ever see your bag again? You are trying! But, if I count right, four trains arrive at the station this day, and none of them has your bag. Perhaps the bag didn't go to Klagenfurt after all. You may have to give up waiting and hoping, and go on without it.

I love the picture of you as a young man sleeping under the hay in a field. In the 21st century, you would call Margaret on your cell phone to tell her where you are and what you're doing. I hope she didn't worry.

July 2

Of course I did not sleep very well but at any rate I kept warm and dry. It clouded up and sprinkled a little about 2 o'clock, but I was completely under the hay so it did not bother me.

Got up this morning at 4:30 and went down to the station. At 5:30 they opened the baggage room but no bag of mine had come in the night. A fellow reluctantly called Salzburg but found out nothing. He then said that the other fellow came to work at 8 and made it very evident that I was to get out until then. So here I sit (6:35) in the waiting room waiting.

11:20. Lucky that I have M.'s key with me so I could get my old sweater from her bag. Also got out "The Meistersinger" to read. However, I was too sleepy to read much.

At 8 the fellow started to call around again. All kinds of trouble because he could not hear. Finally he sent a telegram to Klagenfurt but it did no good as he got a telephone call through. They said they had sent the bag yesterday at 15 o'clock and it should have come here at 22, but of course did not.

Called M. at 9 and told her to go to the station in Salzburg and see what she could find. Also that I would remain here and call her again at 9 tonight or else be on my way there with the bag.

Took a little walk and had my shoe stitched up.

Returned at 10 because by that time Salzburg was to have looked around to see if they could locate the bag. They knew nothing about it but had the slip saying the bag should be sent to Wien when found. Tried to call Wien.

At about 11, in talking with Salzburg they said M. was there and we could talk together. According to M. they have had the bag, but whether yesterday or today they knew not and where it is now they know not. Decided that I stay here and she have them call Wien (as they cannot hear Wien here). When she hears anything she will call here and if the bag comes here I will call there.

Raining now so I cannot go to eat although I am very hungry.

When rain stopped a little went to a place and had an awful meal. So bad I went to another place for beer.

Back to station but no word. Stayed an hour, went away an hour and came back again. Decided to leave on 17.10 so had time for a beer and sandwich.

Just as I left the station for the last time they called me back. It was M. on the phone. She was about to take the next train for Berchtesgaden to bring me some clothes. Good thing she caught me or we would have passed on the way.

In Salzburg, the man said the bag was there, come in at 6. We would not believe it until we saw the bag, but it really was there. I had to pay 3.00 express to get it out. Like a long lost friend. The bag had been sent this morning from Klagenfurt by Personen Zug (*slow, local train*) instead of Schell Zug (*fast train*) and has been on the way all day. Why it was not sent yesterday I do not know.

We found a good room for 5 M. Had a small supper and to bed dead tired.

You are amazing! You never gave up. Your stubbornness, persistence, and patience are qualities that must serve you well as a mathematician. Mathematics requires all of the characteristics you display over the past four days, including tireless detective work and single-minded focus.

I sense your joy in "the return of the bag." Now may the trip proceed.

Later, after finding this journal, I came across another box of notebooks with lists of expenses, photographs, and postcards my parents saved from their trip. On July 3rd, my mother wrote a postcard to a friend describing the incident in detail. She wrote, "After three *exceedingly hectic* days the bag was found last night. It was an awful experience and it was so difficult trying to get the Germans to do anything.... But it came here last night and *are we glad to have it*!"

The postcard is a photograph of the Adolf Hilter Jugendherberge Strub mit Watzmann, where they stayed in Berchtesgaden. I learn that the youth hostel was built in 1935 and that Hitler visited it in 1936.

NOTES

1. During the Third Reich, the German mark was referred to as the Reichsmark (RM); after 1948, it was called the Deutsche Mark (DM). The value of one mark in 1938 was approximately 40 cents.

2. Spector, *Encyclopedia of Jewish Life Before and During the Holocaust*, Vol. 1, 17–18.

3. Ibid., 18.

4. The same youth hostel is still operating today, at a steep 30-minute walk above town.

5. According to the Reich Holiday Law (Gesetz über die Feiertage, February 27, 1934), religious holidays continued to be observed at this time. Source: Anson Rabinbach, author and professor of European cultural studies, Princeton University.

6. Wandervögel (birds of passage) were youth who camped and hiked around the country as free spirits (Guerin, 133).

7. Morris, *Solo, An American Dreamer in Europe: 1933-1934*, 162-3.

8. The National Socialist flag was adopted as the sole national flag on September 15, 1935.

9. Kaplan, *Between Dignity and Despair: Jewish Life in Nazi Germany*, 84.

10. Metelmann, *A Hitler Youth: Growing Up in Germany in the 1930s*, 69.

11. Nixon, *Vagabond Voyaging: The Story of Freighter Travel*, 11.

12. The equivalent of the boys in the Hitler Jugend (Hitler Youth). The teenage girls, wearing uniforms of skirts, blouses, and hiking boots, often worked in factories and on farms. Until early 1938, the farm program, in which city girls were sent to farms for the summer or even longer, was voluntary. Through this rural "program," girls learned how to develop feminine qualities and to prepare for marriage and motherhood. The BDM as a whole was based on Nazi beliefs about women's functions as helpmates to men, bearing children and rearing according to Nazi values, and faithful homemakers (Kater, 73, 84).

13. Metelmann, 162.

14. The mathematician Konrad Knopp, an important analyst of the time who wrote a classic book on infinite series, taught at Tübingen University from 1925 to 1950. He co-founded *Mathematische Zeitschrift* in 1918 and was editor from 1934 to 1952. At the time of this meeting, he was 56 years old. " . . . Knopp seems to have been an upright man who had a conservative distaste for the Nazi hegemony, and who attempted to do his best to maintain his discipline both nationally and as an Ordinarius (*full professor*) at Tübingen in difficult times" (Segal, 263).

15. Bummel: a stroll or "a journey, long or short, without an end" (Jerome, 347).

16. Jerome, *Three Men in a Boat and Three Men on the Bummel*, 288.

17. From "Gillespie Measure," by Anthony P. Morse and John F. Randolph: "In this paper we propose still another definition of linear measure for point sets not necessarily lying on a line. For a point set A we shall represent this measure by G*(A) and call it *Gillespie linear measure* after the late Professor D.C. Gillespie who suggested to us individually definitions similar to the one we have adopted." *Duke Mathematical Journal* 6 (June 1940), 408–419.

18. Liptstadt, *Beyond Belief: The American Press & the Coming of the Holocaust 1933-1945*, 38.

19. Friedlander, *Nazi Germany and the Jews: The Years of Persecution, 1933-1939*, 331.

20. Bessell, *Life in the Third Reich*, xviii.

21. Spector, *The Encyclopedia of Jewish Life Before and During the Holocaust*, Vol. 1, 71.

22. Hegi, *Stones from the River*, 270.

23. The thermal water comes from natural springs in the Florentine Hill in Baden-Baden. "Bathing in the thermal water of Baden-Baden is not only enjoyable, it activates, rejuvenates and stimulates the entire body." www.carasana.de

The Roman-Irish baths at Friedrichsbad were built above the ruins of ancient Roman baths in the nineteenth century and still attract visitors.

24. *Nazi Conspiracy and Aggression,* Volume IV, Doc. No. 1721-PS.

25. Spector, Vol. 1, 203.

26. Gilbert, *Kristallnacht: Prelude to Destruction*, 264.

27. Fuller, *Noor-un-nisa Inayat Khan*, 239.

28. "The Palace is one of finest and most beautiful examples of baroque in Germany . . . ecstatically recommended." *Hand-Me-Down*, 1938. During the war, the palace was bombed and almost completely destroyed but has been restored. There are many baroque statues in the garden, including one for each season and one for each element.

29. "Pension Elite . . . Bunsenstrasse 15, 3 min. from R.R . . . fine service and food, garden meals, English spoken." *Hand-Me-Down,*

1938. In a rare example of continuity, the Pension Elite is still operating at the same location, still provides a good breakfast, and is reasonably priced: this according to Tim and Maxa Burleigh, who provide wonderful, detailed information about self-guided bicycle tours in Germany through their website, www.bicyclegermany.com.

30. Welch, *Propaganda and the German Cinema 1933-1945*, 305.

31. "Bratwurstglockl . . . famous tiny restaurant where Dürer, Hans Sachs and everyone else in Nürnberg and the world have eaten sausages here for the last 525 years." *Hand-Me-Down*, 1938.

32. On January 2, 1945 the thirteenth century Katharinenkloster was destroyed by an Allied air raid; the once beautiful abbey of St. Katherine is now preserved as a ruin known as Katharinenruine.

33. "Nassauer Keller . . . Karolinerstrasse 2 . . . don't miss this and don't let the precipitous stairs scare you off . . . excellent and picturesque, with the best wurst in town." *Hand-Me-Down*, 1938.

34. The 14th century Frauenkirche (Church of Our Lady) is well known for its ornate clock where every day at noon figures representing seven princes parade around Emperor Karl IV. After the war, much of the interior needed to be rebuilt.

35. Friedlander, 87-88.

36. On the evening of June 22, Joe Louis defeated Max Schmeling in Yankee Stadium before 90,000 fans. Louis knocked out Schmeling in two minutes and four seconds.

37. The knight has been played at the Met in the twenty-first century by an overweight Ben Heppner and a large Johan Botha. A *New York Times* reviewer says of the March 3rd, 2007 performance that even though the "hefty" Botha did not look right as the dashing knight, he "nailed it, singing with youthful passion and lyrical nobility."

38. Kaplan, *Between Dignity and Despair: Jewish Life in Nazi Germany*, 46.

39. "Don't fail to see drinking ceremony in Rathaus windows near clock at 11 and 12 o'clock daily." *Hand-Me-Down*, 1938. According to local legend, in 1661 the Protestant mayor accepted the challenge of drinking a jug of wine in one gulp to prevent the Catholic invaders from taking over the town.

40. Evans, *The Third Reich in Power: 1933-1939*, 575.

41. Constantin Carathéodory was a well-known mathematician who made significant contributions to the calculus of variations, the theory of point set measure, and the theory of functions of a real variable. Born in Berlin in 1873 of Greek parents, he had been at the University of Munich since 1924 and was chair of the Mathematics Department until retiring from that position in 1938.

42. "Hofbräu Hause . . . am Platzl . . . beer . . . stupendous place, see all 3 floors . . . beer . . . world famous, packed with about 5000 Bavarians all the time . . . beer . . . never-to-be-forgotten sight and not-to-be-missed . . . beer . . . music Tues. and Thurs. . . . beer!" *Hand-Me-Down,* 1938.

43. "Alte Pinakothek, a jewel of a gallery featuring Dürer's 'Four Apostles.' *Hand-Me-Down,* 1938. This gallery has an outstanding collection of European masterpieces from the fourteenth to nineteenth centuries, featuring work by Fra Angelico, Botticelli, da Vinci, Raphael, Dürer, Rubens, Rembrandt, El Greco, and Goya.

44. "Löwenbräu Keller . . . Siglmaierplatz . . . large garden full of beer, brass band, and sausage . . . solves the food problem forever . . . visit brewery at back." *Hand-Me-Down,* 1938.

45. "Deutsches Museum . . . 9 miles of scientific and industrial progress . . . spend 2 or 3 days here . . . unique . . . This museum has received more recommendations than any item in the notes of any city." *Hand-Me-Down,* 1938.

46. In the revolt known as the Beer Hall Putsch, Hitler, as head of the National Socialist German Workers' Party, was thwarted in his attempt to overthrow the government; he was arrested, tried, and incarcerated for nine months. The actual date was November 8, 1923. Hitler's headquarters, known as Braunes Haus (for the brown uniforms of the Storm Troopers), were on Briennerstrasse between Königsplatz and Obelisk Platz.

47. Segal, *Mathematicians under the Nazis,* 96.

48. Founded by Polish mathematicians in 1922, *Fundamenta Mathematicae* was devoted only to topology, set theory, and foundations of mathematics. It was the first specialized journal in the history of mathematics.

49. *Annals of Mathematics,* a journal of research papers in pure mathematics, was founded in 1884. Since 1933, the journal has been edited jointly by Princeton University and the Institute for Advanced Study.

50. Kac, *Enigmas of Chance: An Autobiography,* 46.

51. Island palace of King Ludwig II ("Mad King Ludwig").

4

AUSTRIA

Note: On March 12, 1938, German troops crossed the border and occupied Austria. Austrians welcomed Hitler arriving in his open car and did not offer military resistance. On March 13, Hitler declared that Austria was now the Ostmark, a province of the Third Reich. Hitler called this first attempt to unite German-speaking people the "Anschluss" (joining together) of Austria with Germany. The American press called it the "annexation" of Austria.

July 3

Sunday. Did not get up this morning until 12. Still raining. Had dinner at the Stiegl-Brau Keller[1] and a good dinner it was. A sort of celebration for M.'s birthday (*July 4*) and return-of-bag day. First chicken we have had since before leaving home. It surely was good.

Got to talking with a young German engineer and nearly missed our train. He is now "arbeitlos" (*out of work*) and taking a little trip before going back to Berlin to find another job. He says there is plenty of work so he will have little trouble finding work.

In Linz, M. stayed with bags while I inquired about the youth hostel. Took train to near youth hostel and M. stayed again while I found it only to find it full. However, they told me where to get a room for a mark apiece: was not bad. Went a different way back for M. and walked past her on the other side of street and then 5 or 6 blocks before returning to find her.

Walked around town and located the boat station.

The sentiments expressed by the young engineer sound very similar to those of a cousin of Henry Metelmann, who had come back to Germany in the hold of a freighter after six years in the "promised land" (America). "He reckoned that he would now find work in his native Germany after the great Adolf Hitler had taken the reins of the state into his safe, strong hands."[2]

After returning to Ithaca, my father received a letter, dated December 12, 1938, from the engineer asking him for a written invitation to come to New York for a short time, "as otherwise the American consul will allow me no visa for visiting in the U.S.A."

In the letter, he states, "Since I saw you so many things have happened in Europe. The Sudetenland is from now on enclosed in the German Reich. Before the Munich agreement (*September 29, 1938*) there were some critical days for the political peace of the world, however, our Führer Adolf Hitler has thank goodness worked together with the other three statesmen, Italian, French, and English (*Benito Mussolini, Eduard Daladier, and Neville Chamberlain*) to again bring about world peace. You also undoubtedly know what a ghastly thing it was, that in Sudetenland so many German laborers were still kept out of the German Reich. One cannot find words to express it. Adults have wept out of sheer joy, wept like small children, because all pain for them has ended."

I found no evidence that anything came of this request to visit the U.S.

Building on the annexation of Austria in March, Hitler was continuing his quest to unite German-speaking people by acquiring the Sudeten region of Czechoslovakia (the Sudetenland), with its three million German-speaking citizens.

As the young German engineer says in his letter, at the Munich conference on September 29, Hitler convinced Italy, France, and Great Britain to agree to the annexation of the Sudetenland. Wanting to avoid war, Chamberlain and Daladier agreed to Hitler's demand that the Sudetenland eventually be annexed to Germany. Chamberlain was hailed as a hero for achieving "peace for our time," but it soon became clear that his appeasement of Hitler at Munich led to the outbreak of World War II one year later.

July 4 (*Margaret's 28th birthday*)

I carried bags to the boat while M. went another way to buy bread, butter, etc. for breakfast and lunch.[3] The day was very nice, being not too bright nor too cold. One little shower about noon. The Danube flows quite rapidly so the boat moves right along. It is a nice ride, but in many ways not as pretty as the Rhine.

The hills are not as high and there are not as many picturesque ruins although there are some good ones. What terracing there is is not as neat as on the Rhine.

The trip is quite long, 9:30—6:30 (*from Linz to Vienna by boat on the Danube*).

We have a booklet of Vienna and a map on which we picked out the spot of greatest density of pensions. Went there by street car. There, however, every person charged as much in marks as they formerly charged in shillings.[4] After looking for nearly an hour I landed in the Hitler Heim looking for the Jugendherberge. No one knew where it was, but one of the men offered me a room in his apartment for 1.50 RM, and I took it. It is Alserstrasse 16, No. 8.

To bed tired and M. catching a cold.

This is M.'s birthday and I forgot to spank her.

So in Vienna, you—my parents—stay overnight in a home owned by a Nazi, or at least a member of the Hitler Youth. I assume he is a Nazi because you meet him in a Hitler Heim, a meeting place or clubhouse for followers of Hitler. I don't know what to think: are you simply desperate for a place to stay, having arrived in Vienna at 6:30 P.M. and spent an hour looking for a cheap room?

It is so easy to judge from hindsight. Would I have stayed overnight in the home of a Nazi? No. But you and I had our differences when it came to politics. I take heart when I read some of your comments in this journal about the current regime in Germany. And I need to remember . . . you are on your first trip to Europe, traveling on a shoestring, and you just want to have a good time! Also, while you don't like the direction the government is taking, you may simply see a Nazi as being a member of the National Socialist German Workers' Party, the ruling party of the government.

If you had taken the boat from Linz to Vienna in August instead of July, you might have seen or at least gone by Mauthausen, site of the "slave labor" camp built by prisoners transferred from the concentration camp in Dachau.

Four months earlier, on March 12, the people of Linz gave Hitler a frantic welcome when he entered the town at the start of the Anschluss. On March 21, *Time* described Hitler's entry into Austria in his large black Mercedez-Benz, along with "a two-mile long procession of German Army and Storm Troops, with six tanks leading the way and German bombers blacking out the sky. Austrians screamed 'We see our Leader! One Führer, one Reich!'"[5] Linz was chosen as a point of entry because of the antisemitism of the people and because Hitler grew up there and considered it his hometown.

The following week *Time* reported on the wave of suicides that swept over "once-gay Vienna" by hundreds of people who would rather take their lives than live under the Nazis. The article stated that since the Nazis quickly took control of the newspapers, news of the suicides was carefully kept from the people.[6]

Almost sixty years later, in 2003, the Austrian government provided reparation checks to Holocaust survivors in an effort to "close a dark chapter that began in 1938 when Hitler occupied the country and forced nearly one million people to work in jobs . . . to aid the German war effort."[7] One recipient describes being forced to clean streets from May 1938 until she left Austria in March 1939.

Spanking on her birthday? I never heard about this practice in our family.

July 5

Walked past the University on our way to the Ring (*Ring-strasse, once the site of the old city fortifications, now a wide boulevard encircling the old city*). Then along the Ring past the Rathaus (*town hall*), Parliament, Natural History Museum, Art Museum, Hofburg (*imperial palace*) and to the Opera. We then walked to St. Stephan's Church[8] along Kärntnerstrasse (the Fifth Avenue of Vienna) looking in shop windows. Went in the church, but felt rather funny because of the almost complete darkness and great number of people praying.

Next walked around locating ourselves and looking at shops. Near the Hofburg we met a Jew who had lived in England most of his life. He came back to Austria several years ago for military service and remained running an office for foreign travel. He had been baptized in the Church of England, and his certificate was signed by Queen Victoria. He was trying to go back to England, but as yet had not received a visa. He piloted us around and we had a little trouble getting rid of him in the end.

About 5:30 we went to a place M. had found in the Hand-Me-Down for petit point bags.[9] They proved to be very interesting people. They are making a bag for her, i.e., putting the already made work on a frame she wants.

It is getting increasingly difficult for Jews to leave Germany and Austria (although, paradoxically, since the Anschluss in March, Austria was expelling Jews across the border). When the war begins, it will be much harder to leave.

I attend a talk by Dr. Carl Rheins at the Chatham Synagogue on the attempts of Otto Frank, father of Anne Frank, to leave Nazi-occupied Holland in 1941. Dr. Rheins, executive director of the Yivo Institute for Jewish Research in New York, explains that Jews had to acquire both an exit visa from their own country as well as a visa from the country of destination. He says that "most likely" the baptized Jew my parents met would have had to go to the SS to request a visa to leave Austria. It appears that he was still an Austrian citizen since he had to return to Austria for military service.

Dr. Frank Mecklenburg, director of research at the Leo Baeck Institute,[10] notes in a telephone conversation with me that in the late thirties "there was no rule of law, no reliability of procedures—clearly, this was one of the things that no longer existed. It is hard to imagine today the restrictions and the amount of paperwork that was required to leave one country and go to another."

In his account of growing up in Nazi Berlin, Peter Gay describes his family's amazing (and darkly humorous in retrospect) route to obtain papers to leave Germany in early 1939. After Kristallnacht, in addition to the "extortionate demands" (surrendering jewelry and other valuables) on Jews to obtain a passport, the regime required not only proof of admission to another country but also proof of guaranteed passage, sometimes dated within a month of departure.

One individual who helped thousands of Jews leave for Palestine in the late thirties was Captain Frank Foley, the British Passport Control Officer in Berlin. A Christian, he has been described as an "extraordinary" man who felt "genuine compassion for those who besieged his office."[11] In a report dated June 1938, he described systematic house raids and arrests of Jews in Berlin and other regions of Germany.

The Quakers also helped Jews escape German-speaking lands before and during the war. With the help of the American Friends Service Committee (AFSC), refugees were able to escape to the haven of the Scattergood Hostel for European Refugees, which operated in Iowa from 1939 to 1943. Aliza Michael Luick-Thomas writes about meeting Irmgard Rosenzweig Wessel in Connecticut: "It touched me that already in

1938 Irm's family found assistance among Friends as she rode the Quaker-supported *Kindertransport* to England, where she lived for two years with a Quaker family before being reunited with her parents in New York and sent to Iowa by the AFSC."[12]

But as early as 1934, the executive director of the AFSC, Clarence Pickett, met in Berlin with Rabbi Leo Baeck to discuss whether there was anything the Quakers could do to "help prevent the barbaric treatment of Jews and to assist the immigration of those who were so fortunate as to be able to go to the United States or elsewhere." In his autobiography, he describes meeting with Rabbi Baeck in Berlin then and again in the summer of 1938; by that time, Rabbi Baeck had decided that rather than try to leave Germany, he would stay to be of service to his people.[13]

July 6

This morning we went to the Hofburg show rooms, but quite frankly I was not greatly impressed. In the afternoon went to Schönbrunn (*Schloss Schönbrunn, a grand palace completed in the 18th century and used as an imperial residence*) and was very much impressed, especially by the gardens. They are so expansive and so well kept. Went through the rooms (45 in number) they let people go through. In the castle there are over 1,000 rooms. Back of the castle, through the gardens and on a high hill is a beautiful columned arcade built only for a nice place to get a good view, and we thought the view well worth the climb.

We next walked (foolishly) to the Westbahnhof (*train station*) to see about schedules and to get tickets. Took the train the rest of the way to the store for M.'s bag. The bag is very pretty, and M. feels most proud of it. Also bought a nice piece of needle point M. had looked at earlier, but left it until tomorrow so the woman can pick out the proper shade of yarn for the background. She is to show M. how to fill in the background tomorrow.

M. caught a cold on the boat the other day and it is worse today.

You write that the owners of the needlepoint store are very inter-esting people. I think Margaret's purchasing a bag and learning needlepoint at the same time is a perfect way for you to meet people as you travel. You are involved in a real activity—not just visiting the sights— and there is a practical outcome as well. I enjoy reading about her interest and delight in learning this new skill in Vienna.

Later, as I was growing up, she sewed most of my clothes. I would come home from school to find my mother hovered over the dining room table with patterns spread out at angles to one another. She'd have me stand at the landing between the first and second floors while she hemmed my skirts. I had to stand absolutely, positively still. "Don't move!" she'd say. I learned to hold my breath and be still. I remember the slant of sunshine as it came through the little window with its four separate panes right at eye level where I stood.

Now I realize that she may have been hurt by my lack of interest in sewing or cooking or domestic life at all. However, she encouraged me to practice the piano for my lessons in-stead of helping her in the kitchen. Coming from a poor family in Lowell, Massachusetts, she valued artistic and intellectual accomplishments and also viewed them as a vehicle for mov-ing into the middle class.

Thinking more about Jewish refugees, I realize that the Evian Conference began on this day, July 6, 1938. With the expulsion of Jews from Austria, and the increasing numbers of Jews trying to leave their home countries, the question of refugees was becoming more and more pressing. The conference, taking place in France, concluded nine days later with no solution, no policy of welcoming Jewish refugees from Germany and Austria, and no condemnation of Hitler's treatment of the Jews. Hitler will interpret this outcome in his favor.

July 7

The fellow where we are staying first said that his daughter would be home next day and we would have to give up the room. She came last night, but still he says we can stay. I had to go with him to the police station this morning to show my passport and answer all kinds of questions.

Had a never to be forgotten experience; a bath in the Diana Bad.[14] The bath lasted from 9 to 12:15. Here it is: Shower, warm pool, warm air, hot air, warm steam, lie down for a rest, hot steam, rub down by a real masseur, shower, lie down in hot air room, lie down in normal temperature room, hot pool, hot shower turning to cold, cold pool, natural temperature pool, walk through cool pool, dried off by a man, pedicure, manicure, lie down on a soft cot in the quiet room for 20 minutes. It was really too much, but was lots of fun.

M. went through approximately the same. Had lunch and went to the art museum only to find we had only 20 minutes as the museum closes an hour earlier than was listed in our book.

M. looked for a sweater and belts while I went to American Express (*on Kärntnerstrasse*) and looked at tripods for the camera.

After we met we went to the store where M. learned to fill in the background on her needle point. Ended up by buying another petit point bag for Mildred (*a friend*).

TRAVELING BETWEEN THE LINES

The climate of suspicion is becoming pervasive now. As foreigners staying in the home of a Nazi, your identity may need to be "verified"—verified that you are not Jewish, most of all.

Why does this sound familiar? Checking the identity of foreigners reverberates today in the checking of Arab-appearing citizens and visitors, the raids and deportation of undocumented immigrants, and the holding back of visas to foreigners—all of this due to a climate of suspicion and fear after the attacks of September 11, 2001. Hitler used a time of "crisis" as justification for breaking the law. The Bush administration used "the war on terror." In Europe as well, fear exists—not completely without basis, but without a coherent, comprehensive response.

Because of my interest in my parents' travels, I continue to read about the thirties in Europe, and, with great sadness and alarm, see parallels here in the years after 9/11—in the gradual erosion of civil liberties, starting in 1933 there, here in 2001 with the USA Patriot Act, the holding of detainees without rights at Guantanamo Bay, and warrantless wiretapping. Americans have seen an expansion of presidential powers, the increasing loss of an independent media, the preemptive invasion of other countries, and the messianic vision of the United States as the rightful superpower of the world. It is alarming how easy it was for the Bush administration to undermine the foundations of our government, solid as they seem to be.

You and Margaret travel freely in the summer of 1938, but the clampdown is well in place by then. On the surface life goes on, and you see little to scare you personally, but simmering below

and about to burst four months later in Kristallnacht is the un-
leashing of the reign of terror in full force.

About the baths . . . I can't imagine either one of you spending three hours at a spa! But what does it mean when one cannot imagine someone else doing a certain thing? Is this a lack
of imagination? Specifically, am I limited by my memories, my
"construct" of my mother, of who she was and what she liked
and didn't like? I may be completely wrong! Perhaps my interac-
tions with her and my interpretation of her gestures only reflect
my point of view, not her reality. Granting that possibility, I let
myself imagine her in her late twenties, lying on a thick, white
towel spread over the pine bench in a sauna, smiling and relaxed.

July 8

Got up early this morning and made the 7:35 train for Innsbruck. We had bought no pictures of Vienna so I took the
bags and went ahead to get a seat. Had some trouble finding
the train as it was hidden on the second track by a train on
Track 1 leaving at 7:50, also with café, for Innsbruck. Since
I had trouble I left the bags and went back to help M. get
on but could not find her. My train started so I had to run
and just caught the last car. This car was a special car with
some 40 boys and they would not let me go forward until
everyone was accounted for. When I finally got to the bags
there was M. also. She had only barely caught the train having jumped on after it started moving. Only by accident she
had learned that the 7:50 train was not the one we wanted.

After all of this trouble we learned that the later train
was a De Zug and by going by Salzburg it would get to Innsbruck nearly 2 hours earlier. We thus got off at the first stop
and after a few minutes wait got on the faster train.

There was an 18 minute stop in Salzburg so M. got off and bought some cigarette holders she had seen earlier and wanted.

The ride from Salzburg to Innsbruck is through some very high and rugged mountains. We got to Innsbruck about 5 so had time to find the youth hostel, eat, see the mountains before sundown and window shop before going to bed.

You had me worried for a minute. Are you going to have a similar experience as the one in Germany when you lost your bag? I think you are extremely lucky this time.

So now I know that my mother smoked in her twenties. I don't clearly remember her smoking when I was growing up, but she may have. Smoking in those days was common…and glamorous. There she was on the train in her long skirt and black felt hat, a cigarette holder in her right hand.

Margaret wearing her
new Austrian sweater

July 9

Today was not very clear and M.'s cold seemed worse so we stayed in town and looked at shops, etc. M. bought a very nice sweater. Could not see much of the mountains because of clouds. I bought a tripod, tripod head, and wire release.

The nice sweater must be the gold wool knitted sweater that I inherited from her! Knowing nothing

about needlework, I take the sweater into our local knitting shop called "The Warm Ewe." The shop owner tells me that the yellow and blue flowers with green leaves are embroidered, and the edging is crocheted. There are antique metal buttons.

The sweater is very feminine, narrowing in a shapely way from the shoulders with tucks to the peplum-like skirt effect around the waist. This rings true because she was feminine and slender in those days, as the photographs show. I am glad to have this sweater as a reminder of my young mother.

July 10

Still raining and M.'s cold is still not better. Wanted to go to Tyrolean dance show but could not get in youth hostel late enough (*i.e., the hostel would not be open late enough for them to go to the show*).

At 10 went to the Volks museum (*Tiroler Volkskunstmuseum—Museum of Tirolean Folk Art*). Old Tyrolean costumes on very realistic wood carved figures. Complete rooms from peasant homes and early stubes (*apartments*) are on the second floor. A guide attached himself to us and we couldn't shake him. Furthermore, he told us nothing and only tried to rush us through.

At 12, went to Hofkirche. Here is the magnificent tomb of Maximilian I (to which he was never brought),[15] surrounded by 12 enormous iron figures of his ancestors and contemporaries. The costumes of these figures are very elaborate. I do not see how such things are made.

In afternoon walked out to Kaiser Franz Josef Strasse (not Kaiser Josef Strasse where we went last night by mistake) to exchange a buckle M. bought in Vienna.

Looks like it will be clear tomorrow.

July 11

The clouds seemed to be breaking away this morning, but they did not do so. Sprinkled and rained several times today. About 5 o'clock the sun came and we rushed out and took a couple of pictures.

This morning I bought a pair of house shoes and M. bought a hat, a kerchief and two belts. We moved to a pension so we could stay out late tonight to go to a Tyrolean show. It was not very good. The shoe patters (*Schuhplattler, a kind of dance by clapping shoes onto the floor to special Bavarian music*) were interesting and different, but the singing was not good, not even the yodeling.

NOTES

1. "Stieglkeller . . . Grand place, below castle—try venison and have it melt in your mouth." *Hand-Me-Down*, 1935. The restaurant/beer garden still exists in Salzburg and is praised for its view and menu. The address is Festungsgasse 10.

2. Metelmann, *A Hitler Youth: Growing Up in Germany in the 1930s*, 70.

3. Linz . . . to Vienna by boat . . . interesting people, fine scenery . . . either bring box lunch or have hot meal on board for 2.20 sh (shilling). *Hand-Me-Down*, 1938.

4. After the Anschluss, Austria changed its currency from shillings to marks. The *Hand-Me-Down* guide was printed in March 1938, so prices were still in shillings.

5. *Time,* March 21, 1938, 18.

6. Ibid, March 28, 1938, 17.

7. *New York Times*, October 16, 2003, B2.

8. Stephansdom (St. Stephen's Cathedral), the Romanesque and Gothic cathedral of Vienna, dating from the twelfth century; the entire roof burned out in the last days of the war.

9. Elsa Ackerman . . . Elisabethstrasse 2 . . . lowest prices for quality petit point bags. *Hand-Me-Down,* 1938.

10. Leo Baeck Institute for the study of the history and culture of German-speaking Jewry, with centers in Jerusalem, New York City, and London.

11. Van Leer, *Time of My Life*, 163–179.

12. Luick-Thrams, *Friends Journal*, June 2007, 7.

13. Pickett, *For More than Bread: An Autobiographical Account of Twenty-Two Years' Work with the American Friends Service Committee*, 93, 99.

14. Today a huge complex with swimming pool, sauna, massage services, and more.

15. The emperor commissioned his own mausoleum but died before it was completed in 1583.

5

Switzerland

July 12

The hotel failed to call us but we made our 7:20 train any-way. In our compartment were two Jewish boys from Vienna on their way to Singen (*at the border of Switzerland*). They had no passes and were going to sneak over the border at night. They planned on going to Paris and there trying to get papers so they could go to America. Before they could get passes from Germany they would have to work for several months on roads or other manual labor and then two years military service. They said they would fight for England, France, or America but not for Germany. However, a Swiss officer and German military man spotted them and took them off of the train at Feldkirch. We wonder what became of them.

Also in the compartment was an Austrian from Inns-bruck and his two daughters. He was most sorry that Ger-many had taken Austria but felt it absolutely hopeless to ever get (*it*) away again.

Later a German couple came in. He is an x-ray expert. They live in Cologne. The woman was quite nice looking and nice. We had quite a heated argument with them about the world situation. We said that all they read was Hitler propaganda and they said all we read was Jew propaganda, so of course (as was expected) we got nowhere. If America would buy machines from them then they would buy food from America. The large families are not for the military, but they do not have enough land to raise food for the popula-tion. The large military is for protection only.

At Lindau we went through the German customs. No trouble at all. They looked at us, asked "Americans?" and did not even look in our bags. *(Lindau is in Germany, just past the border with Austria.)*

Took boat *(across Boden See, Lake Constance)* from Lindau to Romanshorn *(in Switzerland)* and planned to spend our odd marks on lunch. However, the menu was in francs[1] and the exchange so poor that all we could get for 2.58 RM was two weanies and two fried eggs. This with our on hand black bread was our "looked forward to" meal.

The Swiss also did not open our bags.

We went on to Zurich. There I left M. with the bags while I called on a fellow mentioned to us by people in Vienna. Going in the rain I then found a hotel. We bought the *Herald Tribune* and read it in the station hoping the rain would stop, but it did not.

We had a very nice supper (small portions that looked pretty big to us) including potatoes that tasted better than we remembered (after being in Germany) potatoes could taste.

"We wonder what became of them." Oh, what you will learn later! This mild sentence lands in my heart with a thud. Most likely these two young men will be arrested and taken back to Vienna to who knows what fate. At this time, in July 1938, perhaps they will be lucky and only be sent home.

During the late thirties, many German Jews fled Germany through Switzerland. After the Anschluss in March, the numbers of Jewish refugees attempting to cross the border grew largely because Switzerland had historically provided refuge as a transit state. But in the spring and summer of 1938, Switzerland began requiring visas. By 1942, Jewish refugees who were refused entry and sent back faced imprisonment, deportation, or death.[2]

I notice the ease with which you and Margaret travel as Americans. You notice it as well.

You write that the German woman was quite nice. And yet she supported Hitler. I wonder if you asked yourself, "How can she support the Nazis and be such a nice person?" She may have asked herself the same question about you: "How can this nice, intelligent young couple defend the Jews?" Each side thinks that the other has been manipulated and duped.

I am glad to come across this passage about your heated argument. In this trip journal, you don't comment very often on the "world situation."

There may be many reasons for this. I like one offered by my Belgian friend: "Your father may not have written about it much because he knew how he felt about it—he didn't have to write it down." Another reason, she goes on to say, is also likely especially at this time, four months before Kristallnacht and one year before the war begins:

"Your parents may have been very aware of the situation in Germany, but as a tourist you can only say or do so much because social situations have all different angles. It would be like someone coming here and saying, you Americans, all you think about is shopping, there are malls everywhere, and that's what you do in your spare time. And a lot of what poisons a political atmosphere is not always visible (you can't see in this country that about half of the people don't believe in evolution). And they probably didn't listen to the radio or read many newspapers (although your father probably knew some German). So, your parents may simply have followed the thinking of their time. Pointing out the many facets of a person seems to me very rewarding, and trying to understand what moved them so that we can see what we're guilty of in our time."

I find this reassuring and reasonable. Actually, this is one reason why I am having this dialogue with my father.

So today you buy a copy of the New York Herald Tribune. Interestingly enough, the July 12, 1938 issue has very little coverage of events in Europe—and no direct mention of Hitler or the Nazi government in Germany. What might have caught your eye are two items of personal interest.

The first is a front-page story about a speech President Roosevelt gave in Amarillo, Texas the day before. One can almost hear his distinctive voice as he extols Amarillo ("this center of the high plains of the Texas Panhandle") where he was greeted by a 2,000-member band of town and ranch musicians in cowboy outfits. Sounding forward-thinking and 21st century, he spoke about his farm program to conserve water, restore grazing lands, plant trees, build ponds and lakes for damming of rivers, and encourage small farming and local food growing. All of this was to help "tie down" the top soil of the Panhandle, one of the hardest-hit areas of the Dust Bowl. You would often tell others that you came from the Panhandle of Texas, and Amarillo.³

The second front-page story with a personal connection concerns the round-the-world flight of Howard Hughes in a twin-engine plane, named the New York World's Fair 1939. Hughes and his crew had left New York on July 10, landing in Paris 16 hours later. Theirs was the second trans-Atlantic flight from New York to Paris after the first completed by Charles Lindbergh, flying the Spirit of St. Louis in 1927. Growing up, I heard stories of your father, Albert Clyde Randolph, particularly the one related to Lindbergh's flight on May 20–21, 1927.

My grandfather was the worker at Ryan Aircraft who had the idea that a periscope would help Lindberg navigate since the pilot could not see directly ahead of him as he flew; when the idea was accepted, my grandfather installed the Aeroscope.

I am sure this story interests you for another reason: as reported on the front page, the Hughes aircraft is fitted with modern radio equipment that is proving to be extremely useful for long-distance communication. Having just spent two years at the Institute for Advanced Study, you must feel you are living during a time of new and exciting communication technology.

This issue includes only a few items of world news. One states that Great Britain is losing hope for an early peace in Spain, and another reports on clashes in Palestine, with bombs, stabbings, and battles between guerrilla bands and the military throughout the "land which Great Britain proposes to divide between Jews and Arabs—to the dissatisfaction of both."

Two pieces refer to the possibility of war in Europe. In his column, "Today and Tomorrow," Walter Lippmann analyzes the impoverishing effect that preparing for war has on the economies of European countries. He writes, "We are witnessing what is in effect a prolonged and total mobilization of all the people of Europe. . . ." The other is a news item reporting that Dr. Nicholas M. Butler, president of Columbia University and head of the Carnegie Endowment for International Peace, has returned from a visit to Europe where he spoke with more than 200 statesmen. He has high hopes that there will be no general war, that the people do not want it, and that it will occur only as a result of governmental policy. Unfortunately, Dr. Butler proves wrong on all counts: he also predicts that there is no chance that President Roosevelt would run for a third term.

July 13

It is still cloudy this morning and looks little like clearing up. The ride to Linthal was quite pretty. The train goes close to Zurich See and the view reminded us very much of Ithaca. At Ziebruche we changed to a little local that took us through Glarus to Linthal. At Linthal one bus left in 11 minutes after the train arrived, but the clouds were so low that we decided to wait for the next bus at 13:44. If it does not clear up by then we will spend the night here and go on tomorrow (if it is clear then).

When we got to Linthal (*seems to be written later*) it was very cloudy so we decided to at least wait for the 13:44 bus. Walked out of town a little way. The clouds would clear away and we would think that surely we could go. Then in 10 minutes it would be all cloudy again. Clouds would clear away in one part of the sky and we would get glimpses of very rugged high snow capped peaks that we never suspected were there.

For lunch we ordered one "mitagessen" (*noon meal*) and the portions were so large we both had plenty. When the bus left it was sprinkling so we stayed. Got a room for 4 francs (*about $1*) and went up and took a nap.

Woke up about 4 with the clouds pretty well cleared and prospects for leaving tomorrow good. About 5 we started to climb to the Braunwald (*a resort*). The trail is very good but quite steep. Part way up we met a man with some goats and took some pictures of them. Got some very good views of the valley and mountains. However, before reaching the top (it took a little over an hour) it had clouded over and was sprinkling. In a sheltered place at the hotel we ate some bread, green cheese, and chocolate we had along and waited 1½ hours for the rain to stop.[4] The way the clouds would evaporate, form again, rise above us, or sink below was very interesting. Finally we started down in a sprinkle. Went to bed with little hopes of leaving tomorrow.

The last settlement in the main Linth valley is Linthal (653 m / 2,142 ft; pop. 1400), with mighty mountains rearing above the little town. Selbsanft (3,029 m / 9,938 ft) lies above the artificial lakes supplying the Linth-Limmern hydroelectric scheme, with the Gries glacier; the Bifertenstock (3,426 m / 10,722 ft) and Tödi (3,614 m / 11,858 ft). Tierfehd, 5km / 3mi south is a good base for walks and climbs.

Lake Zurich, with the Alps in the background, must remind you of Cayuga Lake in Ithaca, with its multilayered terrain of hills and gorges. I know you plan to return to Ithaca and Cornell after your two years away at Princeton.

Since you are writing for yourself and Margaret, you don't need to explain what is obvious to you. To me, it sounds like you want to take a bus up through a spectacular mountainous area and are waiting for it to be clear so you can see the views. What else in this journal do you not write about because it is obvious to you?

I learn that the small town of Linthal is surrounded by tremendous mountains, the highest in the Glarus Alps being Mount Tödi (3,652 meters high). It is amazing to me that you are climbing up into these Alpine passes. Braunwald, still a resort today, can be reached by funicular or on foot, as you do on your way to the Klausen Pass.

I assume you like the green cheese only because you don't write that you don't. I like reading about the food you eat and the combinations of food you like: chocolate with bread and cheese is an excellent choice.

July 14

Woke up at 5:15 with sky nearly cloudless so was very happy. At 6 you couldn't see a thing for clouds. However, by 8 it was again clear so we decided to go and at 9 it was beautiful.

The ride was extremely beautiful and I have enjoyed it more than anything I can recall for a long time. The way the road skirts around the side of a cliff (occasionally ducking into a tunnel) is marvelous, but no more marvelous than the driver's driving. He never slows up even for the sharpest curve or narrowest road and keeps his musical accompaniment horn going, but he makes you have full confidence in him by his efficiency.

The highest point on the pass is 1,952 m.

A little beyond the pass we stopped for 1¼ hours for lunch. M. and I had our own lunch for which we were glad as the meals at this little place cost from 3 f. up. Took a little walk and took a picture of peasants working and mountain as background.

The road skirted around a cliff with a tremendous drop. Looking down it was almost as if you were in an airplane. The peasant houses looked like doll ones and the people themselves were dots. Moreover this lasted for some distance. And looking straight across the valley and up were great snow capped peaks.

At Altdorf the driver stopped by the statue of William Tell (in the main square of the town). Flüelen is very close and we had an hour there before the boat left.

Lake Lucerne is, I am sure, the nicest lake I have ever seen. The water is a light green (very much like Fayetteville Green Lake), the mountains rise right out of the water, and the little towns are all like pictures. The boat goes right past the place where William Tell is supposed to have shot the apple.

Lucerne (*Luzern*) itself is very pretty even though it seems to consist mostly of hotels.

I left M. with bags and found a very nice room. After supper (1 for 2) we walked along the water front and then window shopped. After dark many of the buildings, a covered bridge, and a fountain were all nicely lighted. Then an absolutely full moon came up over the mountains across the lake to make the picture perfect. Had a beer (not as good as German). Went around to see the Lion of Lucerne (commemorating the lives of men from Lucerne lost in 1792 trying to save the life of Louis XVI)[5] which is lighted at night and then went to bed.

Similar to island weather, this region's weather is changeable by the hour, affecting your decision to stay in Linthal or go by bus up into the mountains. Just like the mountains themselves, the weather is mysterious. In the 21st century, you would be able to check online, even watching webcams of the mountains' summits, but you are dependent on your own observations and guesses and the predictions of the landlady.

Again, you are reminded of a lake in New York State. Fayetteville Green Lake,[6] a glacial lake surrounded by forest, is just east of Syracuse, where you and Margaret met each other earlier while at Syracuse University. I like the thought of you as a young couple—a young instructor and a college student—going for an outing at the state park.

July 15

Had thought of taking the boat back to Flüelen but got up too late to get a boat to make good connections. I took a picture of the Lion and then we had to rush to make the 10:40.

The Swiss trains are marvelous. They are so clean and they go to such unbelievable places. This train stayed very close to the lake nearly all of the way, going into tunnel after tunnel to do so. Stayed on the train to Göschenen and changed there for a cog road to Andermatt. From the map it looks like the other train goes to Andermatt but this is because it goes through a tunnel almost directly below Andermatt.

At Andermatt M. saw to getting the bags on the bus and I went into town and bought bread, ham, and chocolate.

We thought Andermatt was high, but the bus goes much higher to get over the Furka Pass.[7] The weather was perfect and we had fine views of the mountains. There was a 15 minute stop at the Rhône Glacier. The glacier is very rough and the light blue and blue green was very pretty. There was however a lot of dirt on top. A very steep drop to Gletsch. Took a picture there.

Everyone except M. and me got off at Gletsch but others got on. The rise from Gletsch to the Grimsel Pass is even more steep than any of the others we have been on. The peaks are also more rugged and there is more snow. Soon after we reached the top clouds began to form. During the stop at Hopiz the sky was completely covered and we seriously considered staying there, but went on. We were not sorry as we could see fairly well and the clouds were pretty.

Part way down was a towing car that had evidently been crowded off of the road and must have turned over several times. It could not have been done more than 3 hours earlier.

At Meiringen we took the train to Interlaken Ost and there had to wait 20 minutes for a train to ride the 5 minutes to Interlaken.

Supper and to bed with orders to call us at 6 if it is clear.

July 16

They called us at 6 but it was not our idea of being clear. However, we got ready and started. The trip up to Kleine Scheidegg was very pretty but the clouds still looked threatening. At K. S. we did not go directly on, but walked up to Eigergletscher (glacier). There it looked like it would clear up so we took the next train on up.

On the way they stop at two stations (Eigerwand[8] and Eismeer) where you can look through windows at the valleys below and the mountains across. On top we could see down the valleys and some of the peaks, but it was not too clear. Fixed and ate the rest of our lunch. It began to cloud up and was soon snowing. Took some pictures of a couple of girls we met on the way up. Later on it cleared up pretty well so we got some more good views.

The railway tunnel stations on the way up and the hotel at Jungfraujoch certainly are wonderful engineering feats. When you get off the train at Jungfraujoch (underground) you walk one level into a room where cards and trinkets are sold, and then on outside to a balcony from which you get a good view of Jungfrau and little peaks close by and to the left the beginning of the Aletsch Glacier. From this room an elevator takes you up four stories (one whole floor a dining room) where you go out through a tunnel to the open snow on the plateau. Walking over the plateau a distance you can look down the other way toward Interlaken. We never got a very good view this direction, but the sheer drops and rugged rocks sticking out of the snow were very spectacular. Occasionally there are rumblings caused by moving ice in the glaciers or snow and ice dropping over cliffs.

60 feet under the plateau (with an entrance up above) is an ice palace. The plateau is solid ice, as the guide said, a stationary glacier. The guides have carved the palace. It consists mainly of a skating rink some 75 feet long and 35 feet wide with 2 large pillars supporting the roof. Also there is a bar room with bar, tables and chairs and piano carved from the ice all electrically lighted by wires hidden in the ice walls. The ice crystals are very pretty, so delicate and clear. They form everywhere.

Back to where the train stops. A tunnel to walk through (over 700 feet long) leads out to a plateau and gentle slope where they have polar dogs to pull you in a sled (at 1 frank apiece) and where you can ski (skis 1 f. boots 2 f.). Along the tunnel are side tunnels one leading to the tourist haus, one to a scientific institute, and a third to the Sphinx elevator (1 f.).

We stayed until the last train that would make connections to Interlaken (4:30 and it left right on time). The way back does not entirely reverse the way up as from Kleine Scheidegg. The connection is to Grindelwald instead of to Lauterbrunnen. On the way down we talked with some of the members of an organized party from Texas. They are going to 10 countries in 40 days.

It was raining in Interlaken Ost, but we started the walk home anyway. Bought fruit, bread and butter on the way in.

Just as we were going through Interlaken the clouds lifted and the sun shone full force on the Jungfrau. The darkness of the valley where we were and the bright sun on the white snow made a very pretty sight. I tried a time exposure and hope it comes out. During the time exposure a fellow stopped to see how I was doing it. He turned out to be a professor of English at Western Reserve (Foster by name). He is very much interested in photography and has already taken over 200 feet of film in his Leica in the 3 months he has been over.

To bed dead tired.

In Switzerland, you are meeting more Americans than you did in Germany and Austria. But 10 countries in 40 days! This is not your style, or mine because you passed yours on to me. To take this trip, with all of its arrangements, you and (mostly) Margaret must have planned it thoroughly. You seem to know where you want to go next and what you want to do. She will pass on an interest in travel planning to me as well.

There's something to be said about going every year to the same vacation cottage on the lake—unlocking the porch door, remembering how one locked it the previous September, having the feeling of continuity—but we never did that. My mother felt that the world is large. It waits for us with new places to visit each trip we take.

July 17

Were rather lazy this morning so did not get up in time to catch the 9:30 train but waited for the 12:03 one. Even though this is Sunday, all the stores and shops (even American Express office) were open. Quite touristy. In one of the wood carving shops we bought a very nice little musical cigarette case. When the box is opened it plays two tunes, Rose Marie and Die Blaue Donau (The Blue Danube). However, when we got to Zermatt M. unwrapped the box to try it and the darned thing would not work. We wrapped it up and are sending it back and hope to get our money back.

The train skirts the Thunersee to Spiez. These Swiss lakes surely are pretty, so blue and clear and the hills and mountains close by so nice. The train goes through all sorts of tunnels in its effort to stay along the pretty shores.

At Spiez we changed for a train to Brig. This ride is the most spectacular train ride I have ever had. A long train of nice comfortable immaculately clean coaches with clear plate glass windows polished until you can't tell that they are there, rushing over a winding, twisting, betunnelled, but fairly smooth road bed under the power of two electric locomotives. The views are marvelous and the best part is that you see most of them two or three times from different levels as the train winds back and forth up a mountain side. There is at least one place where the train goes in a mountain, makes a 180 degree turn and comes out higher up going in the opposite direction. Also on this route is the next to the longest tunnel in the world, the ___, ____ miles long (*Simplon Tunnel*, 12).

At Brig we again changed, this time to a little local (Personen Zug) affair. Moreover it was very much overcrowded, so we could not sit down even after they put on another car. The passengers were nearly all mountain climbers, or at least walkers. There was such a crowd we thought we would have trouble getting a room (in Zermatt), but I found one in 5 minutes (for 4 f.) in a private house. We are on the third floor and have a marvelous view of the Matterhorn.

The day has been nice and clear so we have had some wonderful views. Coming up from Brig it was unbelievable how some of the peasant houses are perched up on the top of high cliffs or on steep mountain sides. Then there are little churches, nice and white with a cute little steeple, stuck up in the most isolated places.

The trip from Interlaken to Zermatt is only 4 hours 23 minutes.

There are no cars in Zermatt, the only approach being by rail or foot, so all the hotels have big horse drawn stagecoach affairs. The streets are narrow and everyone gets out and walks up and down in the evening.

July 18

Slept until we were ready to get up this morning. About 9 we had the pack sack all packed and ready to go for a walk. However, we spent an hour buying walking sticks (which turned out to be a big help). They are light (in color and weight), have a curved handle, a spike in the end, and an Alpine Rose with the name "Zermatt" carved on it.

We walked out of town toward the south and then up a trail through the trees to the left. In about an hour we had reached the little hamlet of Findelen. We walked on a little farther toward the Findelen Glacier and ate our lunch at the highest point we reached.

All during the climb the Matterhorn was to our backs, but we stopped often to take in the views. We went down the same trail we had come up so had good views all of the way. We were very lucky as at no time did clouds cover the Matterhorn and we understand that this is the first day for some time it has not been covered most of the time.

Had a new film put in the camera.

Your walking sticks are beautiful. The wood is smooth and worn, the Alpine Rose still clearly visible. I am so grateful to have one of them, a tangible link to you, my young parents, adventurous and hardy walkers in the Alps.

Because you are so self-reliant and independent, I wonder why you need to have someone else load the film into your camera. Then I see from your Leica manual that loading and developing the film in spools was a delicate procedure with instructions for daylight, subdued daylight, and a darkroom. At home you take care of this yourself, but while traveling it is certainly easier and safer to ask a shop to do it.

July 19

Our landlady was to call us if the weather looked clear. At 6 A.M. woke up and discovered it was perfectly clear so we got up and rushed out by 7. The landlady's barometer had fallen a little so she expected clouds and bad weather.

The climb we made was to Gornergrat (10,280 ft.)[9] and we made it in the 4 hours it is supposed to take. We were both surprised at how easy the climb was. A very good path, broad and well graded, leads all of the way up. Clouds formed in the valleys and it looked rather bad at times. Met a very pleasant Swede on the way up.

On top the weather was perfect, with just enough big white fluffy clouds to make things even more beautiful. Mt. (Monte) Rosa (15,200 ft.), the highest peak in Switzerland, is very close, the Gorner Glacier is all that is between. Also across the glacier is spread out a great range with the principal peaks, Liskamm (14,680 ft.), Pollux and Coster (13,870 and 13,400 ft.) and Breithorn (13,675 ft.). Then over the valley looms up the Matterhorn which is 14,770 ft. high, but looks higher because it is so steep and no other peaks are near it.

We stayed up until nearly 3 (although there is no water on top) and were down about 6.

During the day I suspected that something was wrong with the camera so took it into a shop to find out. It turned out that we had taken no pictures today. We certainly were sick. The person who loaded the camera last night had done it incorrectly. The woman who owns the shop gave us a new film, 4 good pictures from Gornergrat and developed a roll of film, but even so we are still sick. It was the nicest place for taking pictures and we had taken extra pains with them.

Not having the pictures you took "extra pains" with is a loss. You did an amazing thing this day—climbed a mountain in the Swiss Alps—and now you will have no record of the experience. You feel "sick"—not a word often used today in this way—meaning disappointment, regret, anxiety, with a little dread tossed in.

At home, my father developed his own photographs, and he took good care of his camera equipment, as he took care of everything he owned. His attitude was, "I have this bicycle, or this lamp, and, therefore, I need to take care of it, keep it oiled, and in good running order so that it can serve its purpose for as long as possible." He once told me that he still wore the sandals he had bought twenty years earlier in Beirut. He liked things to work and to last.

July 20

This morning we started rather late for a leisurely walk on the other side of the valley from the two previous walks. Had a little trouble finding the way, but when we did find it it went straight up. We went to what is called Hohbalm (8,600 ft.). It is not a peak but a high flattish place from which are many fine views. It is just north of Matterhorn so we got a new view of this peak.

Margaret striding on Hohbalm

We could look almost straight down to the little hamlet of Zermatt. The little houses grouped so close together looked so small and helpless.

We returned by way of Trift, the upper part of the trail going just below two large glaciers.

Our little easy stroll turned out to be quite a long hike.

July 21

Had the landlady call us this morning at 6 and started out at 7 or a little after. First went up the regular trail to Schwarzsee. We were a little more tired than usual so it took us a little over the 2 hours it is supposed to take for the trip. Had tea there (at 1.20 a portion).

The trail from Schwarzsee to Belvedere (*a hotel*) is rougher and steeper than the trail to Schwarzsee. In fact the last half of the trip is right up and although the trail is broad and pretty well graded, there is danger of falling rocks. Also if one became dizzy he could get a real fall from almost any place on the trail.

The view from Belvedere is the most spectacular we have had. The peak of the Matterhorn is so high and so straight above you. There were people climbing but we could not see them. The hotel is 10,800 feet above sea level.

We walked only a little above the hotel in order to see the snow on the north side of the Matterhorn.

Met a couple of English med. students and they walked all of the way to Zermatt with us. In returning we took a trail to the left (instead of going on to Schwarzsee). Went down a long lateral mountain of an old glacier. There was no vegetation and underfoot were small loose stones. Each step you would slide a couple of feet extra so we made headway fast.

The trail then went down a steep grainy slope into the trees. There the trail split into many trails and the one we took soon played out. However, we went in the direction we knew to be proper and soon picked up another trail. This one led, as we had hoped, through the little village of Zermatt we had seen from above yesterday. Looked in the tiny chapel which seemed too small for use. There were no seats, only kneeling benches and they're very close and made of rough boards.

Were surprised that we did not feel more tired when we arrived home.

July 22

Did not take a hike today although the weather was perfect. Went up on a hill and sat in the shade watching the peasants gathering their hay. They have a systematic way of putting a big pile on a rope, tying it, getting it up on a man's head and he walks sometimes ¼ mile or more, up a ladder and pushes the hay through a door into the loft.

Haying

Later we walked through the little cemetery where many of the guides and men who have been killed by falls from the peaks around Zermatt have markers. We also went through the gruesome little museum where they have pictures of those who have fallen and shoes and bits of clothing that have been found. The keeper is an old guide and mountain climber who lost the fingers of one hand and toes of one foot by frost bite while ascending a peak in Peru.

Margaret resting by the Matterhorn

July 23

We really should have gone on today and I wish we had. However, we had no pictures from Gornergrat so we decided to reclimb that. The weather was beautiful when we started, but clouds began to form and soon covered Matterhorn (we had taken some pictures farther down which we hope more than ever are good).

As it turned out there was no point in going clear up so we turned off only 5 minutes from the top and went toward Grünsee. The rain caught us in a little while, but we were lucky in finding a good overhanging rock. In an hour the rain stopped so we went on. Ate lunch during rain.

Tried to find some Edelweiss but were unable to do so although we walked a long distance from the trail. I found a knife out there though.

Walked up to the Findelen Glacier and took some pictures. Came on down the streams formed by the glacier to Findelen and then to Zermatt. A good walk, but on the whole an anticlimax.

I am sorry the walk was an anticlimax. How often we try to repeat an experience, either duplicating a pleasurable one or trying again one that didn't work. Such an effort is doomed to failure, I think, since one is in a different moment the second time. As it turns out, one of the pictures you take becomes a favorite of mine: the one with Margaret seated, looking up at the Matterhorn. So it was worth it after all.

July 24

This morning when I woke up it was raining hard. I got up and went out to see if any (*people in*) costumes came to church, but nothing very good came in the rain.

The landlady had a little wagon to take our bags to the station which was a help. The train was very crowded and the clouds were low so the trip to Visp was somewhat of a disappointment. Also it is supposed to be pretty all the way to Montreux, but I'm sure we could not see all of the mountains we should have.

In Montreux I found a room without much trouble. It was too far to carry the bags so we checked them and took only the pack sack. Washed up and went for a walk. Suddenly M. discovered we did not have our canes. We rushed back to the station and there they were where we had left them (lucky).

By paying 20 cts. (*centimes*), we got the poste restante money order for the music box we sent back to Interlaken. However, my hat was not there.

Montreux seems to be mostly large hotels. The lake front (Lake Geneva) is very pretty. All along the water front is a nice walk lined with trees and flowers. The hotels have wonderful lawns and flowers. Took a long walk along the walk.

Again, you don't explain that you lost your hat. You don't expect that your journal will be read by anyone other than you and Margaret, so there is no need to explain something you know.

Your willingness to take the time to return the defective music box pays off! I will hear this message from both of you: send in those coupons, call if a bill doesn't look right, follow through with what you have started, and you will be rewarded.

July 25

Went to the P.O. again but no hat.

The train, which was little more than a trolley was very crowded at first. It wound back and forth 6 or 7 times going up the hill back of Montreux. An hour after we started, we could still look down to where we started. A good many got off at Les Avants (a resort). We had room to eat our breakfast.

At Montreux we changed to another still smaller train (one car and baggage-locomotive) *[called a char-à-banc in Hand-Me-Down]* and got off at Gruyères. I had the conductor put our bags off at Bulle so we could later walk from Gruyères to Bulle (because this would simplify some complicated connections).

Gruyères is up on a hill top and still surrounded by the old wall. The women were out in the main street washing clothes at the fountain on a big board on which they pounded the clothes. We took several pictures among them the ancient measures (*grain measures carved out of a stone block*). Later had luscious strawberries and real whipped cream at the Hotel de Ville (*recommended in Hand-Me-Down*). Got so interested in the place we allowed only 35 minutes for the walk to Bulle.

The day was hot and we walked like mad to make the train at Bulle. Just as I ran into the station the train pulled out. We were very disappointed.

There was a very accommodating agent at Bulle and together we figured out a route. Went way down to Chatel-St. Denis, over to Romont, where our ticket to Fribourg [Freiburg] was good. He gave us allof the extra for the amount we did not use going to Morat (Murten).[10] As it happened we went on to Basel instead of stopping at Bern. Of course we missed Morat and were sorry for that. It turned out better in the end though as it took 3 hours to get RR tickets for France in Basel and we would have had only 20 minutes otherwise.

Had the heck of a time finding a room, and finally came back and took one nearly across the street from the station.

Spent our last Swiss money on fruit.

NOTES

1. The value of one Swiss franc (100 centimes) in 1938 was approximately 23 cents.

2. *Switzerland, National Socialism and the Second World War: Final Report*, 105.

3. His alma mater, West Texas State Teachers College, was in nearby Canyon.

4. Alpine areas, with their "rich and lush pastures" are known for their cheeses, among them a green cheese known as Sapsago. Unique to the Swiss, it is green-grey in color, hard, and has a pungent spicy flavor. It is produced in the mountains of the canton of Glarus, Switzerland where it was invented by monks in the sixteenth century. www.cheesemonthclub.com

5. Löwendenkmal, a dying lion hewn out of the side of a cliff to commemorate 700 Swiss mercenaries killed by French revolutionaries, just off the square.

6. A meromictic lake, which shows evidence of ancient plant and marine life because there is no fall and spring mixing of surface and bottom waters.

7. "Alt. 2431 m. The Furka Pass is the highest shelf of the great longitudinal furrow that divides the Swiss Alps from Martigny to Chur." *Michelin Guide, Switzerland*, 1991, 90.

8. Only eight days later, on July 24, 1938, the Eigerwand (Eiger wall) was climbed successfully for the first time. In an article in the *New York Times* on July 25, the author, noting that weather forecasts in the Jungfrau region are always unpredictable, reports that the climbers are feared dead. *The White Spider: The Classic Account of the Ascent of the Eiger* by climber Heinrich Harrer describes this climb of the mountain's north face.

9. "Don't miss this no matter what inconveniences . . . finest panorama in Switzerland . . . 10.000 ft., top of the world with the Matterhorn aglow at 4 A.M. *Hand-Me-Down*, 1938.

10. Called "Morat" by the French-speaking minority (12%) of the town, but known as Murten by the rest, mostly German-speaking residents.

6

FRANCE

July 26

They did not even open our bags in the customs office. Got a good seat on the train, a whole compartment to ourselves. The train was steam drawn so was dirtier, but is heavier and rides easier than any of the Swiss trains. Went back to dining car to see about lunch and noticed a regular second class coach with temporary third class markers so we moved in and had a much more comfortable ride.

Had lunch (or dinner) on the train and it was swell. We had forgotten there was such good food. Things are looking up.

Menu:

1. Hors d'oeuvres (sardines, cold ham, pickled cucumbers, cauliflower with bread and butter)

2. An excellent and large chop, scalloped potatoes, green peas. Seconds for everything.

3. Selection of half a dozen cheeses and generous portions.

4. Fruit and nuts.

Price including 10%, 57 frs. or 1.71 for both of us.[1]

Back to the compartment full and satisfied. I took a nice nap.

Arrived in Paris at 2:30. M. went to an information office and obtained a couple of maps of Paris. She then stayed with the bags while I went in search of a room. Hotels listed in the Hand-Me-Down for 28 and 30 frs. for double room were as much as 60 frs. The Hotel Molière was 55 for example (*listed in Hand-Me-Down for 35 frs.*). These hotels were, however, in the central part of town (not far from the Opera). I next walked between the Louvre and Les Tuileries, over the Seine to Rue de l'Université. Here I also found prices high. My wanderings next landed me on Boulevard Saint Germain and I located the Hotel Taranne with double room for 23 frs.

Went back to Gare de l'Est for M. and bags and we got to the hotel and cleaned up by 7. Rue Monsieur le Prince (on which the Oldenburgers[2] live) seemed not far so we started there. However, we did not have much money so I took the Metro to the Opera (*Metro Opéra*) to get more at the American Express and M. went on to find the Oldenburgers. I got the money at the Grand Hotel (A.E. being closed) and returned to meet M. and O's at Les Deux Magots. There we had a Raphael sec (very good) at 4 frs. each. Later went to a restaurant (rather expensive), then stopped for some champagne (small portion and not too good for 2.25 frs.) and then went to O's room.

The O's pay only 17 frs. a day and we can have their room tomorrow as they are leaving in the morning for a trip in Switzerland and Italy. They showed us some good eating places and gave us other advice. Finally left them at 12 o'clock.

I am amazed at how easily you navigate Paris. You seem completely familiar with it and quite at home. This must have come from studying the map and reading up on the famous landmarks. I am thrilled that your wanderings landed you on the Left Bank, in a hotel that is next door to Brasserie Lipp, where Ernest Hemingway often went in the 1920's.

The nearby Les Deux Magots, is also a favorite café for artists and writers. As young mathematicians, perhaps you and Rufus Oldenburger carry on the tradition of intellectual discussion over your Raphael sec. How I would love to know what advice the Oldenburgers gave you about Paris and if you talked about current events in Europe.

It appears that they are renting an apartment in Paris. In your first entry in this journal on May 28, you wrote that he came over on the freighter with you and then took the train to Paris, but you didn't mention a wife. Perhaps she is French? Or she was already in Paris? This is one of the mysteries I have to accept in reading your journal.

I have my own memory of Les Deux Magots. Many years later on a trip to Europe with my son Nash, then 15 years old, we went to the famous café to have coffee with Daniel Karlin, a French filmmaker and friend of a friend. He told us that he used to meet Jean Paul Sartre and Simone de Beauvoir at the café, and that his first lover left him for Simone!

In two years, the Germans would invade and occupy Paris. The novel, *Suite Française*, opens in June 1940 with an air raid on a hot early spring morning. In her notes to herself when writing this book, which was based on her own experience, Irène Némirovsky listed scenes she wanted to describe for posterity. The first three are:

1. Waiting in queues at dawn
2. The arrival of the Germans
3. The killings and shootings of hostages much less than the profound indifference of the people

On July 13, 1942, Irène Némirovsky was arrested in her home and deported to Auschwitz, where she died a month later.

July 27

Coup de Maussens (?)—M., Muscat—J.—wines at lunch.

We told the people at the hotel we would move and they seemed not to mind. Had breakfast (standing up, it is more expensive to sit down) of excellent coffee au lait and pastries for 2 frs. apiece including tip. Then went to a coiffure where M. had a shampoo and wave set and I a hair cut. Moved over by taxi. Had lunch at a prix fixe at about 28 c. apiece. Looked at shops in the afternoon and went to an English speaking movie.

July 28

Went to the Louvre. Bought a guide book and had one heck of a time finding out anything from it. Finally located ourselves, but it was too late to see a great deal. Had an awful meal in an awful place.

In afternoon we separated and M. looked at belts and bought gloves and I just walked around (spent a good deal of time telling men I did not want any dirty pictures and did not want to go to any *such places*). Met M. at American Express and we walked out to the [*left blank*] district. Had supper there at a not too bad prix fixe.

July 29

Walked out to Sacre Coeur and had an excellent view of the city. Later went to the very poor play, Oscar Wilde (his life and trial).

I wonder what you don't like about the play, or was it the performance itself? Oscar Wilde, by Leslie and Sewell Stokes, was

performed in London in 1936 and will have a very successful run in New York City beginning in October 1938. Perhaps it is too modern for your taste.

July 30

Late start (as usual). Damned hot weather, don't feel like getting up early. Ate lunch at Pam Pam (across street from Opera). Took films to be developed. Bought gloves (at Perrin's) and rushed to Catacombs but it was closed. Had champagne at Deux Magots. Home and fooled around.

Margaret, wearing hat and smiling, next to John at far right

Does "fooling around" mean what I think it does?

The Catacombs with its underground network of tunnels and walls of bones became the headquarters of the French Resistance during the war.

July 31

About 10:30 we walked down to the Louvre and stayed there until after 2. Then walked out along the Seine. It was very hot. Went to Hotel des Invalides and around the large grounds to Napoleon's Tomb. Then walked over to the Eiffel Tower and went to the first platform. Next walked to Arc de Triomphe and by luck got there just in time to see a ceremony at the grave of the unknown soldier.

August 1

I went to the American Express while M. stayed at home and wrote letters. The idea was that I get schedules to Versailles and Chartres and we go on one trip today. However, there was such a rush there that I could find nothing. Phoned M. and she met me and then did some more shopping. I bought tickets to the Opera for Wed. night (Faust) for 19 frs. apiece.

Later we took the Metro to Hotel de Ville, walked around there a little and then over the bridge to Notre Dame. Next walked to the Place de la Bastille where of course only a monument marks the spot. Bus back to Hotel de Ville and there took a boat on the Seine. This was a very interesting ride (only 3 frs. apiece). All the way past the Exposition (mostly torn down) to Mirabeau where we took the subway back.

On a park bench near Notre Dame saw a man most certainly dying from syphilis.

The man dying of syphilis must be a shocking sight to you. Undiagnosed and untreated, as he most likely was before the widespread use of penicillin, this man is probably covered with rashes, perhaps blind and paralyzed, uncoordinated, and demented.

Today the neighborhood of Notre Dame contains a site that was not there in July 1938: the Mémorial des Martyrs de la Déportation. When Farid and I visited it in 2004, we read about it first in our *Lonely Planet* guide to France: The Memorial to the Victims of the Deportation, erected in 1962, "is a haunting monument to the 200,000 French people—including 76,000 Jews—who were killed in Nazi concentration camps during WWII." As we walked down the steps into the darkness, we found ourselves with others who also wanted to hear what this underground memorial said to them.

August 2

Took the train this morning at Gare Montparnasse at 8:31 for Versailles. (Prisoner chained to an officer and white man with negro wife and baby on train.)

At Versailles we walked through the magnificent gardens to the Grand and Petit Trianon. Met a Frenchman who showed us the garden of Marie Antoinette that we would not have found by ourselves. The day was very hot and it was a relief to get out away from the Paris streets.

Later we returned to the Palace and went in. At first it was very uninteresting. We walked through room after room with absolutely no function and only big pictures on the walls. Finally, however, we came to the Hall of Mirrors in which the Treaty of Versailles was signed. There was no function here either and all of the chandeliers had been removed, but by asking a guard we found the exact spot where the treaty was signed. The Hall of Mirrors at Herren Chiemsee is much more impressive.

Also of interest were the rooms of Louis XV through which you have to go with a guard. The furniture is left in these rooms. We were more interested in the rooms of Marie Antoinette. They seem so small.

After walking on to the Gallery of Battles (where the armistice was signed) we went outside. Took a few pictures and then looked for a place to eat.

Rushed to the station to catch the 2:42 train only to find that this train runs only on Sunday. Had to wait until 3:48 for a train. It was a modern, aluminum stream-lined affair, but had very poor ventilation and was hot as the dickens.

Got to Chartres at 5:31 and rushed for the cathedral for fear it closed at 6. However, it was open and stayed open as long as we were there. The cathedral has two spires, but they are not twin spires. The architecture is very nice and the cathedral most impressive. It is not as large as Notre Dame, but we liked it better.

A fellow tried to pick M. up when I was in a different part of the church.

In France (as in America) many fingers, noses, heads of small figures of the statues are missing. One thing about Germany, there seems to be no such vandalism.

In the twenty-first century, a "white man with negro wife and baby" would not be cause for comment. Little did my father know that his own daughter would find herself in the opposite situation: a "white woman with an African-American husband and two babies." Coming from Texas in the first half of the twentieth century, he reflected the culture in which he grew up. In the 1970s, when I became involved with the man who would be my first husband, I had to correct him: Dad, it's not Negro anymore. Say "black." He listened and accommodated. But he never truly understood his daughter's political and social choices even though he had no trouble at all loving his beautiful grandsons.

Your experience upon arriving at the station and learning the train to Chartres will be later than you expected—and then finding the cathedral open and liking it very much—sums up the angst and pleasure of travel. You make your plans, hope for the best, panic when things go wrong, and arrive (or not) at your destination, settling into whatever happens.

I am not at all surprised that "a fellow" tried to pick up Margaret. She is lovely with her big eyes and delicate features.

At the time my father wrote this entry, there has been just one Great War. My father doesn't even mention the name of the war that was finally ended with the Treaty of Versailles, signed on June 28, 1919. It does appear he was wrong if he thought the armistice for World War I was signed at Versailles since it was signed in a railway car in Compiegne Forest. He may have been referring to the armistice signed at Versailles in 1783 between Great Britain and the United States.

August 3

M. did some more shopping and I went for the three rolls of films I left to be developed. We will have some fine pictures.

While eating lunch we saw the two girls we met going up the Jungfrau. They wanted to see a night club and so did we so we planned to go after the opera. They got opera seats for 4 frs. apiece.

After lunch M. bought some handkerchiefs and then I went home while M. had her hair fixed. Had to rush through supper to get to the opera by 8. The opera house is magnificent, much more impressive than I expected. Our seats were very good, second row of 4th balcony and near center. We could hear and see nicely.

After the opera we met the girls by appointment and went to the Sphinx. I was disappointed. The women wore nothing above the waist and had little on below, but they were fattish and none of them were good looking. There were many people in the little room and everyone was hot and sticky, and a victrola[3] (not good reproduction) blazed away. The girls all looked tired and their tactics were far from alluring. As we left one girl with absolutely nothing on was standing on the stairs. She was too drunk to know much of what was going on.

So you go to two operas on this trip! This is the Opéra de Paris Garnier, the elegant opera house in the "royal" center of Paris. How wonderful that you do this, and how appropriate that you saw the French opera by Charles Gounod. It's fun that you meet the two girls (women?) you hiked with in Switzerland. I can just imagine your reaction at hearing they spent so much less for their tickets bought at the last minute.

August 4

Were of course very tired today. I went to American Express about noon to see if there was any mail and to leave a forwarding address.

At noon a telegram came from the Canadian Travel League saying a boat would sail from Hamburg on the ninth. This we did not want so wrote them so. Even though we had no sailing we decided to go on to England in the morning until we remembered that we have no English visa.

August 5

Went to the British Passport Office this morning and got the visa. It is near the Arc de Triomphe so I took a picture of the tomb of the unknown soldier. Walked all of the way home just to get my last good look at Paris.

A letter came this morning confirming the telegram of yesterday and saying they strongly advised our taking the reservation as no other boats were going from England or the Continent for some time.

Slept in the afternoon and did a little packing.

You must be worried about getting home. The telegram from the Canadian Travel League is dire. In September, the U.S., France, and England will be urging Americans to return home as soon as possible, but the fear for Americans' safety is already apparent in August.

After Hitler's speech in Berlin on September 26 demanding that Czechoslovakia cede the German-speaking Sudetenland to Germany, Europe and the U.S. became alarmed for the safety of Americans traveling abroad. It appeared that war was likely.

That day, the State Department issued a warning to Americans not to go to Europe, and for those already there to make arrangements to come home immediately. Referring to the "difficulties being experienced by Americans in obtaining immediate passage home," the announcement "strongly" advised Americans not to travel abroad.

In London and Paris, the U.S. embassies issued this statement:

> "In view of the complicated situation prevailing in Europe, it is considered advisable to recommend that American citizens who have no compelling reason to continue their sojourn here arrange to return to the United States."

The *New York Times* reported that hundreds of Americans were deluging shipping offices in Great Britain and that steamers in the next few days would be fully booked. It noted that for "some time" U.S. Navy vessels had been sent to the waters near Great Britain to be ready for Americans in an emergency evacuation.[4]

In Paris, the *New York Times* reported that the "obvious signs" that France was preparing for war, coupled with the statement from the American Embassy, led to a "rush for departure" among Americans on both ships and trains. Hundreds of people visited or called travel agencies and steamship offices. Americans also crowded into banks to withdraw funds and into the American Express office to deposit valuables.[5]

However, adventurous travelers that you are, you continue on to England despite having no passage home booked. To me, this sounds like a combination of a desire to continue this first amazing trip abroad and denial of the events unraveling around you.

NOTES

1. The value of one franc in 1938 was approximately 3 cents.

2. Rufus Oldenburger was a mathematician (Ph.D. 1934, University of Chicago) who also had been a member at the Institute for Advanced Study in Princeton. He traveled with John, Margaret, and friend John Kludt to Europe.

3. By 1938, "Victrola" had become a term commonly used for the type of phonograph designed by the Victor Talking Machine Company.

4 "Warning by Hull on Travel Abroad," *New York Times*, September 28, 1938, 17.

4. "Americans Urged To Leave France," *New York Times*, September 26, 1938, 11.

7

ENGLAND

August 6

We're called this morning at 6:45 and got in a taxi at 7:45 for the north station. Had a big argument with the driver as his meter read 3 frs. before we even started. Then he went a very zig zag route to the station, but he had us as he knew we were in a hurry.

The whole station was overrun with people. Everyone seemed to decide to leave Paris today. Got two seats on the very dirtiest train in the world. It was crowded to the very limit and was late in starting.

However, we arrived in Boulogne nearly on time. Had a ham sandwich and cup of coffee and rushed to the passport office. There was an enormous crowd there and there was absolutely no control; everyone pushed and shoved. We were there a half hour and got out on the dock only to find another such crowd and had another push and squeeze to get on the boat. There was no place to sit so we climbed up on a pile of life preservers until it got too cold and then we jumped the fence and went in the first class compartment and sat.

Another crowd and push to get off only to find that we had to go back on board to get some passport card. A lot of people had to do this and were just as mad as we were. The customs line was mobbed, but M. got in some way or other and the fellow didn't even open a bag, the first break we have had today. However, the train to London was jammed full so we had to wait for the next. We got on this train but it also was crowded to the gills. We got two seats and rode quite comfortably to London, Victoria (*station*).

Leaving France

In London M. tried to call the Canadian Travel League (although it was 6 o'clock) and failed. We then checked M.'s bag and the black bag (on which the handle had again broken) and went across the street to eat. Paid 3/4 (3 *shillings 4 pence*)[1] apiece for supper, the highest we have paid for a meal since leaving home. The food was good, but the portions small. We then took the underground for Highgate and then a bus a bit farther and walked quite a distance to the hostel.[2] To bed dead tired.

If it is this crowded on August 6, think what it will be like in another month. Some of the crush may be attributed to the annual desire of Parisians to get out of the city in August. But it feels ominous and more serious than the usual race to leave town and go on vacation.

Again, you two, on your first trip to Europe, amaze me at how confidently you find your way around a new, huge city. You take the underground to a neighborhood in North London and then a bus to the youth hostel, all after what sounds like an extremely stressful day.

I notice that you call the Canadian Travel League upon your arrival in London.

One year later, in September 1939, England and France declared war on Germany. Then, as vividly described by Janet Flanner (Genet) in her letters from Paris in *The New Yorker*, Parisians definitely evacuated Paris when they moved south with their belongings. In the fall of 1940, with the Blitz on British cities, people would be leaving London as well.

Sunday, August 7

Had a real breakfast of cornflakes, bacon and eggs, bread, butter, marmalade and tea. 1/-. Miss Savory and her friend came over soon after 9. We can use her bike, but not the other girl's brother's. Bill Savory joined us and the other girl left us and we went to Trafalgar Square with its statue of Nelson. From there we walked down the Mall to Buckingham Palace. It had started to rain. We were late to see all of the changing of the guard but saw some of it. The rain spoiled some of it as the guards wore capes over the nice red uniforms and had their flags rolled up.

Margaret, center, in her "rain cape," with
friends at Number 10 Downing Street

Next went to 10 Downing St. and were impressed with
how plain it looks. Went around by the Horse Guards on
Whitehall and then to Westminster Abbey.

After that Miss Savory left as she is a nurse and had
worked all night. Bill took us around to a place across the
street from Big Ben for lunch. It was now raining quite hard,
but we went to an Underground and as close to the London Museum (*Museum of London*) as possible. However, it was
hard to find and we were soaked by rain before getting there.

The museum is all about London from early Roman
times and was very interesting. We stayed there over three

hours. We then found the Canadian Travel League office and then we went home, Bill leaving us at the station.

Had supper at the hostel for 1/- each.

It appears that you quickly made some new friends who live near the hostel, or were they referred to you by other travelers or Americans at home? "Miss" Savory—how quaint that sounds now, or perhaps her first name is Miss.

At the end of your notebook, you write down the names and addresses of a man and woman and scrawl in the corner: "couple at Highgate Hostel traveling on double bike."

You make sure to find the Canadian Travel League office. It is clear how important this is to you.

Monday, August 8

After our hostel duties were over M. went straight to the Canadian Travel League office and I took the bags we are using to the Central Youth hostel and met M. at the C.T. L. They promise us a passage within 10 days.

We went to the National Gallery and spent some time there looking at the early Dutch and Flemish paintings.

On our way to lunch we had fun feeding the pigeons in Trafalgar Square and taking pictures of each other doing so.

Ate lunch in same place as yesterday and then went to the Tower of London. Close to the Tower we saw large crowds of men in a small square. It is a place of free speech, as we were told, and men talk or do anything they please and then take up a collection. One group was watching a strong man stunt and another listening to a fellow talk. In the Tower we went in the Bloody Tower (*the square tower in the Tower of London famous for murders of princes*) but did not go to the jewel room.

John with pigeons at Trafalgar Square

Later M. went to do some shopping and I walked through the financial district around Cheapside and King William Street and walked over London Bridge.

Had supper at the hostel.

I can just see my mother going straight to the Canadian Travel League office. She could be very determined when she wanted something. Within 10 days is quite a range. Will it be tomorrow, the next day, next week? Where will you get the promised ship?

This is one of the few entries where you describe your experience in a personal way. In uncertain times, you and Margaret do the kind of thing people enjoy—feed the pigeons in Trafalgar Square.

Tuesday, August 9 (*no entry*)

Wednesday, August 10

Did practically nothing either day. Saw Canadian Travel League, walked around, etc.

Thursday, August 11

Breakfast was delayed this morning so we did not get as early a start as we should have. Went to Canadian Travel League office, but they had no further word. I then went to Victoria Station for M.'s bag and the black bag while M. looked up bus fares. We then met at the Paddington Station. There we found a bench and spread our stuff out and made up a pack for the sack and put everything else in the bags. We changed clothes in the public toilets. Then sent the three bags to Swansea (*Wales*) and with the pack started out.

After a little lunch we took the bus (Green Line). Asked the conductor for a map, but he didn't have one and suggested that we buy one. He stopped the bus by a store and told us to go in and he would hold the bus. They didn't have a map, but who ever heard of a bus being held like that?

Another thing, we didn't know exactly where to buy our tickets for (that is why we wanted the map), so by the time we had decided to go to Guildford we had gone some distance. The fare from where we got on was 2/6 but from where we were at the time we decided it was 2/3 so he charged us only 2/3.

At 2:30 we got to Guildford, but it was nearly 3 before we got to the edge of town. The very first car we motioned to stopped to give us a ride. He took us only about 3/4 mile, but it was up a hill and was a help. The next ride also was only a short one.

We then had quite a long wait. Car after car went by without much indication of stopping. A chauffeur going the opposite direction asked if we wanted a ride and a woman going in the opposite direction made motions as if she might return for us. Later she did return and picked us up.

She was going only about 6 miles and before it was over she asked us to stop for tea. After a little holding out we accepted. She drove in to a regular estate, tennis court and all. The great big dining room table was all set for tea with little sandwiches, shrimps, and several cakes. The husband came in soon with a friend. They had been playing golf on his private 9 hole golf course. I had a very pleasant talk and some wonderful tea. The friend took us on to Farnham.

At Farnham we picked up a 4 or 5 mile ride. Then an Army looking truck came by and offered us a ride and of course we could not refuse. They turned out to be the King's Royal Rifle Corps. Soon they dodged into a little side road, turned a corner and stopped. We started to pile out, thinking the ride was over, but they said "to stop up" and they would take us on as they were only dodging another truck. They then took us all of the way to Winchester and then turned around and went back.

The hostel is a very interesting place. The building was built in 1744 as a mill and is one of the landmarks of the town. There is a stream that flows directly under the building and is divided into two channels for two water wheels. Now, however, one channel is used as a wash place for girls and the other for boys. You dip a pail in the stream and pour the water in a wash basin. Or if you want a bath you just jump in the stream and hold onto a rope to keep from being swept away. It was cool but lots of fun. The sleeping rooms are directly above the streams so you hear the rush of water as you go to sleep.

Jack Chamberlin of the Princeton Gym team was there. We also met a young couple from Connecticut who are also having (or did have) trouble with the Canadian Travel League.

It was a beautiful evening. After supper we walked down the main street of town. The buildings are very old. We walked around the old cathedral (*Winchester Cathedral*) which was very dark and still until the pipe organ began to play softly. A full moon added just the right touch for a romantic stroll along the little narrow winding streets close by.

Well, you certainly seem to know what you are doing. The Canadian Travel League must have told you to go to Swansea in Wales to get your passage home. You even know how to send on your bags so you can travel freely on your way there. And now, in addition to ship, boat, train, bus, and bicycle, you can add hitchhiking to your methods of getting around.

This was such a day of adventure—one of those unexpected treasures that can happen when traveling. What a gift to be in-

vited to the estate, tennis court and all. Both of you being tennis players, it must have been tempting to get out there on the court.

My father's colleagues at Oberlin College, where he joined the mathematics faculty in 1943 (and where I was born), remember well how passionate he was about the game. "Fuzzy" (Elbridge Putney) Vance, mathematics professor, and Bill Renfrow, chemistry professor, recall that my father was always ready to get out and play. He taught me how to play, always reminding me to "keep your eye on the ball." This turned out better than the lessons in arithmetic and geometry.

The King's Royal Rifle Corps, with its unique historical roots in the American colonies, will be deployed to Europe during the war. "Of course we could not refuse" sounds like you might have wanted to refuse, but I don't know why. However, your ride sounds unique— mysterious and comical.

Although they may not hitchhike to get there, young backpackers still go to Winchester today. Until recently, the hostel still operated within the building called the Mill, a National Trust property built over the River Itchen.

Friday, August 12

This morning we walked down to the cathedral again but were inside only a few minutes until a service was to start so we had to leave or sit down until it was over. Next we went to the museum at the only remaining main gate of the old city wall. After that we went to the old castle (*Winchester Castle*) and saw King Arthur's round table. It is on a wall where it has hung since the 17th century. We were lucky in getting there no later than we did as the city council meets in the next room and visitors are not allowed in at the time of meetings, and it was only a few minutes until a meeting was to take place. It was too bad we could not stay longer in Winchester as there are many other things to see there.

Our first ride was a short one, but the next one was a nice long one, some 50 miles or so clear past Wimborne Minster (*church begun in 1050, in town of Wimborne*). This was with a surveyor who specialized in (*treating*) damp walls.

Another ride or two and then we got in with a caterer with 200 lbs. of ice cream and cake, and he took us to Dorchester. Some time or other a woman by herself picked us up and she was the one who said so often, "You make me laugh." Our last ride took us to the outskirts of Exeter so we walked about a mile to the main post office.

There was no telegram there.

As I was putting the pack back on, an oldish looking fellow unexpectedly lifted it for me to help put it on. He was very friendly and started to talk and soon invited us out to his house to tea. He is a most interesting old fellow, 82 years old, but very wide awake and active. He is a retired builder, but keeps up with a sort of building loan association. He preaches every Sunday at a small village church nearby and has done so for 60 years. He bought some old houses near the railroad that no one else would have, fixed them up, and rents them to poor laborers for 5 shillings a week. He has bought a confectionary business and is giving it to an Austrian whose wife is part Jewish. This Austrian has a Ph.D. and is now a private tutor in Czechoslovakia and cannot return to Austria. Frank Charby (the old fellow) knows the Austrian will not be good in the confectionary business but he only wants them to get a start here.

We had a nice tea. His wife, much younger than he, had only returned today or they would have had us stay the night. We took a picture of their house, very cute, with them and their dog Bingo. After tea he insisted on taking us to the hostel in his car and came in to look the place over. He knew the house from boyhood. The children (*literally, of the youth hostel "parents"*) were at supper and he started right in talking to them and gave them demonstrations of dove calls that amused them very much.

The hostel is 2 miles out of town in an old house that at one time was a most wonderful place.[3] The hostel was started only this spring but is very comfortable.

How fortunate you are to meet this delightful "oldish" man. I remember you being 82 years old, also considered a "most interesting old fellow." But that comes later. Now you are 34, and Margaret is 28. Thanks to compassionate people like the old man, some are saved during the terrible years ahead.

The Austrian Ph.D. and his Jewish wife find themselves in the opposite situation of the Jewish man you met on July 5th in Austria. They want to return to Austria but cannot; he is in Austria and wants to return to England but cannot. Yet their predicament is the same: because of their Jewish identity, they cannot live where they wish to live.

"There was no telegram there." You set this off from your long, descriptive paragraphs. It is a stark and lonely statement.

Saturday, August 13

Walked a couple of hundred yards out to the highway and almost immediately caught a ride the 1 mile to Exeter. Went to the P.O. but no telegram. M. looked for a tea cozy, at Irish linen and Harris tweed. I looked for a pipe and had my dark glasses fixed. After we met we went back and ordered a piece of tweed to be sent from Leeds to Swansea. They say that it should get there by Tuesday and we hope it does.

We then bought some little cakes for our lunch and went to the cathedral (*Exeter Cathedral*). This is a very large and old cathedral, part of which has been standing as it is today since the 12th century.

About 1:30 we got out on the highway with ideas of going to Torquay. However, after an hour of waiting a fellow going to Dawlish stopped so we went there instead. There are interesting red sandstone cliffs there, but the beach is not good and the railroad runs between the beach and the city. We started on down toward Teignmouth, but a little sprinkle started up before we got out of town so we turned back.

Our luck seemed to have turned as we got only two short rides in 2 hours. After walking a long way and getting sprinkled on, M. decided to take the bus in. I walked on and within 2 minutes got a ride and beat M. home by quite a good deal.

They still had room and meals for us at the hostel for which we were glad. In the evening had a nice talk with a young German (Hans R. Goldschmidt) (*his London address written at the back of the notebook*) and a Canadian from Hamilton.

It is ironic that my father describes Exeter Cathedral in terms of remaining as it was since the twelfth century. Only a short time later (in the long view of history), in May 1942, it would be seriously damaged during the bombing of Exeter. Again, as so often revealed in this journal, I notice that my parents traveled in a world that no longer exists—in terms of customs, attitudes, costs, and places that were as yet not damaged or destroyed during the war.

Sunday, August 14

After waiting a while for a ride, we took the bus to Exeter. Walked to the edge of town and in a very few minutes were picked up by a preacher (H. Hitchman) on his way to hold a service at a little outlying town. He had traveled quite intensively and was interested in what we are doing. He took us some 12 miles or so to beyond Copplestone.

Again we had only a short wait until we were picked up by Mr. C. H. Cunliffe, Corybus, 20 Gills Hill Radlett, Hertfordshire. He had had asthma for 13 years and could not get out of bed. Dr. Francis of London had cured him 18 months ago and he has had no trouble since. He took us to Barnstaple, waited while we saw about a reservation at the hostel and took us on to Ilfracombe and said he would take us to lunch if he were not going to lunch with some other people.

We arrived in Ilfracombe after traveling 56 miles, at 12:15 just 3 hours after leaving the hostel at Countee Wear (*on Countess Wear Road in Exeter*)..

At Ilfracombe we climbed a high hill that overlooks the town and border on one side and the sea on the other. The coast is very rough and rocky, looks like granite.

Later we went down the hill to the town and got a little to eat. Ilfracombe is a very touristy place although not a very fashionable one.[4] We found that the price of the ferry to Swansea is 5/6 but it costs 3d (*pence*) to get onto the pier where the boat docks. We later learned that it also costs some more to get off of the pier at Swansea.

About 4:30 we started back and picked up a ride with two women before we had even stopped walking. They were local women and, as we had already heard, speak a local dialect, and use such expressions as "us thinketh it won't rain today." They took us all the way to Barnstaple.

The woman at the hostel jumped all over us for going in the hostel earlier, but cooled down when we did not talk back at her. She probably thought we were German at first since we have German cards and I had left them. Could not get a warm supper in town.

Here you show your awareness that Germans are not popular in England at this time. Although you don't mention conversations about "politics," you must know that the British are passionately anti-Nazi and pro-peace.

August 15

There was no telegram this morning. We got $10 changed (to 2.0/4) (*2 pounds*) and looked at some interesting sheepskin rugs. Around 11 o'clock we were out on the road trying to get a ride to Clovelly. The first ride was with a local fellow in the lumber business who lives 3 miles out. He has been to London only once in his life and says he knows only about 20 miles around Barnstaple. The next ride was with a young couple who took us to (*left blank*). M. did not like it because I read a book of theirs most of the time. After walking to the edge of town we got a ride all the way to Clovelly. This was lucky as Clovelly is 2 miles off of the main road.

Clovelly is a nice little fishing village that is built right on a high cliff. It is very pretty and should be run with only the natives, but there were 10 times as many tourists as natives.[5] They overran the place and every house is turned into a tea room. We had a wonderful tea of tea, rolls, butter, Devonshire cream (*a clotted cream*), strawberry jam, and cakes for 1/3 each.

Coming back we walked for a mile or so along the narrow little road leading out to the highway and then got a ride with a man, woman and dog all of the way to Barnstaple.

There was still no telegram. We washed up, bought some bananas and went to a show.[6]

My parents' travels out to the countryside remind me of the many children who in a few years would be evacuated during the bombing of London and other cities in England. Elisabeth Grace, a friend and fellow Quaker, writes, "I spent the war years ricocheting between various families in the relatively safe English countryside and my own increasingly unfamiliar home. When things quieted down in London, I was brought home; when the frequency of air raids increased, off I went again to a new address." As a consequence, beginning in 1939 at the age of five, she spent about four years living with various families and attending different schools with each move.

Preparing for war entailed drastic measures: "I was told years later that the old woodshed at the bottom of the garden was quickly stocked with 'tinned' (canned) goods, and how our neighbours, a family of four brilliant at mathematics but sadly lacking in common sense, had buried vials of cyanide in their vegetable plot in case the feared German invasion necessitated suicide." For a while, Elisabeth and her grandmother slept in a "Morrison shelter," a huge steel table turned bed that was designed to withstand a direct hit in an air raid.

NOTES

1. The value of one shilling (12 pence) in 1938 was approximately 25 cents.

2. According to the Hornsey Historical Society, 136 Tottenham Lane, London, this was likely the youth hostel in Highgate West Hill, which was the residence in the 1800's of an assistant judge, a Lord Chief Justice, a mayor, and an architect.

3. The Exeter Youth Hostel has a web page with a photograph and description on the Youth Hostel Association website: www.yha.org. uk. The house dates from the seventeenth century.

4. "Full of trippers . . . better go on to Isle of Man." *Hand-Me-Down*, 1935.

5. "One of the quaintest and most unusual towns fast being spoiled by tourists . . . take least possible luggage as descent from road is steep and donkeys scarce." *Hand-Me-Down*, 1935.

6. They probably went to Albert Hall, which was used for concerts, theater, and cinema in Barnstaple.

8

Wales

August 16

There was a letter from the C.T.L. (*Canadian Travel League*) this morning telling us that there was a ship at Swansea fixed for the St. Lawrence, but there was nothing definite about her sailing date. We decided to go on to Swansea and be there in case there was a sailing soon.

Looked at raincoats for me, but did not buy one. Also looked at sheepskin rugs and did buy one. It took a lot of deciding, but we finally got it. It makes a big roll to tie on the top of my pack.

About 3 o'clock we got out on the road for Ilfracombe and soon got a lift all of the way in and got there a little before 4. We knew that a boat left for Swansea at 5, but found at the boat office that the boat goes by way of Tenby and is a 5 hour trip instead of a 2 hour one. We decided to go anyway.

The day was windy, the water rough, and the boat small, and that is a bad combination. People began to get sick 5 minutes after we left and I believe that absolutely everyone was sick before we got to Tenby. M. was terribly sick. I was mad at myself for getting sick only 10 minutes before reaching Tenby. At Tenby we decided to get off and make it to Swansea the best way we could. It was then 8:15, the boat being 45 minutes late.

Tenby is a small resort place and this is the height of the tourist season. We could find no room in Tenby and anyway they charged 6/6. We started walking out on the road and even though it was nearly dark a fellow picked us up. He was a local fellow and took us to a farmer's where we got bed and breakfast for 4/ each.

The farmer and his wife were very funny to us and probably we to them. They said that they generally got "only respectable people—not that you are not respectable." Our room was one of the smallest in the world. The pack took up most of the available floor space. She finally put a puff on the bed saying she guessed that we would not hurt it.

You seem to have no choice but to go where the Canadian Travel League tells you to go. You must be very worried about getting home. Not only do you want to get home, but you need to get to Ithaca to teach in the fall. On the other hand, I can't help but be impressed by your confidence that soon a ship will be sailing from Swansea and your determination to get there in case it does.

August 17

The first ride this morning was with a couple of women who asked us to ride with them. It was on a curve at the top of a hill and I had not motioned because it was a bad place to stop. They let me out right by a Gypsy camp and I thought we would have a hard time getting another ride. However, a car had to slow down when the women stopped and as I motioned to him, he took us in and we went right on. He took us to Carmarthen. On the other side of Carmarthen a priest picked us up. He was going only a little way, but took us on down the road 5 or 6 miles and I am sure if his family had not been expecting him at home he would have taken us all of the way to Swansea. He had a very unnatural laugh, but I am sure his pleasure was genuine. Two fellows then picked us up and took us to within 2 miles of Swansea. They went a different way to Mumbles (*the seaside village of Oystermouth, also known as the Mumbles*).

M. mentioned what good time we had made and then discovered that she had left her Zermatt cane in the car. She stayed with the pack and I hooked a couple of rides to see if I could locate the car. I walked all over Mumbles and the little peninsula on which it is located, but did not find the car.

When I got back (in about 1½ hours) I found M. well taken care of. The people in the cottage at the corner had provided her with a stool and she was sitting there reading her paper.

The fellow was only spending the day at Mumbles so we thought that he must return by our corner. So I stayed with the pack and M. went to Swansea to see if there was a telegram and find out about boats, etc. We made the arrangement that if she did not return by 6, I would meet her at the general post office at 6:30. The lady at the corner let me use the stool M. had used. At 5 o'clock she brought me tea and cakes. The tea was served in a coronation cup for Edward XIII. She looks on the present king and queen as sort of substitutes but feels that the English people would never have accepted Wallis as queen.[1]

At 6 o'clock I went into town and met M. at 6:30. She had been around to different offices to see about passage. She learned that Willowpool was in dry dock, would not be out for several days and would then have to load after that.[2] The Cragpool was loading but the passenger list was full.

Most of the boats from Swansea are booked through James German & Co., but they had nothing in the near future that could take us. Their Yorkwood left last night and the Maplewood is to leave tomorrow night. Also M. had been to the office of Holder & Bros., and the men there had taken her to see the captain of the City of Boston. He did not carry passengers, but might have been persuaded to take us if he had not been taking his wife and daughter on the trip.

We wrote a card to Nyveen (*agent at the Canadian Travel League office in London*), telling him that if he could not give us definite passage by Sat. Aug. 19, to return our money. Found a room in an awful dump, but even so the landlady highhatted us like the major domo of the Waldorf Astoria. Supper of fish and chips and to bed.

August 18

After an awful breakfast of boiled eggs we got to the P.O. about 10:30. M. went to Couch & Co. office to see if they had anything, and I went to Holder & Bros. office as they were phoning around to see if they could find a boat. They told me of the Blair Athol sailing from Port Talbot for Quebec tonight, but said she did not carry passengers. The agents are G. _____ Lewellyn and M. _____ (GLM) in the Pembrook Bldgs., Swansea. Also they found the Maplewood sailing tonight full up and the Cragpool tonight or tomorrow also full up.

We called at the P.O. at 11, when we were to hear from Nyveen if he had anything, but there was no word. We then put in a call to London and asked Nyveen if he would give us passage on the Cunard line for £15 but he refused so we instructed him to forward our money to us at Swansea.

We told a man at the P.O. our troubles and he said to try T.W.R. Mason on Somerset Place and a fellow named Burges in Queens Bldg., who is some sort of immigration officer. At Mason's I started in by saying "We have been having trouble with the C.T.L., and he immediately began to smile. He said that we were the eighth ones to come to his office with the same complaint. One fellow was told to come to Swansea for a boat that sailed 2 days earlier. Mason advised that we go to the G.L.M. office and see about the Blair Athol even though she did not carry passengers.

At the G.L.M. office they said their office in Port Talbot (*in Swansea Bay*) was the only one that could say. They then called their Port Talbot office and that office said that everything was up to the captain and that he would be in their office at 3 and they would ask him. We decided to go to Port Talbot and see what we could do.

We then had only 24 minutes to make the train so I ran all of the way to the room and threw the things in the knapsack so we would not have to pay for the lousy room again. I just barely made the train. The train is very slow and stops at every cross road so it took 35 minutes to make the 9 miles to Port Talbot.

At Port Talbot we found the G.L.M. office and they said that they could do nothing until they saw Captain Macdonald, and said he would be in at 3. However, it was then only 1:45 and time was getting short so we asked where the Blair Athol was berthed and how to get there. We had to walk ½ mile or so, take a little dirty water taxi (for 2d apiece) and then walk a couple hundred yards to the ship. Climbed a long dirty ladder to get on deck which was dirty as could be with coal dust. Found Captain Macdonald in the salon sitting over a glass of scotch with a customs officer. He said the ship did not take passengers, which of course we knew. We told him our hard luck story and he said that he could make room for us and that as far as he was concerned we could go, but everything would depend on his owners in Glasgow. He was going back to town pretty soon and would phone them, but would give us no encouragement. He said that if we got the big boss on the phone he would be nearly sure to say no and that it was according to how the junior partner felt what he would say.

Anyway, back in the office of G.L.M. they called Glasgow and they said we could go at 10 bob (*shillings*) apiece a day so I guess they got the junior partner and he was feeling good. They then made out papers for us and we signed a couple of papers. The captain went back to the ship (and took our knapsack and roll with sheepskin rug) and told the steward to make a place for us. The captain then came back and we went to the customs house and signed on as members of the crew. Agreed to be on board ship at 8 o'clock sober and in good condition.

It was then about 4:30 so we caught the first train back to Swansea to get our bags and things. Had only 1½ hours until the train for Port Talbot that would get us there before 8 o'clock. M. went to the P.O. and sent some cards and I rushed all over town trying to find a store where I could buy a raincoat. However, Thursday afternoon is a holiday in all of these towns and I could find nothing open (*"half-day holiday" for small shops that are open on Saturday*). Grocery stores and bakeries were open so we bought some chocolate, mints, chewing gum, oranges, and cake.

At the station discovered that the top of M.'s bag had been sprung down and caught. The top was weakened, but not broken. We made a fuss about it, but could get no satisfaction. It was not until later that we discovered that my bag was actually broken. I am sick about it, but can do nothing now.

Took a taxi from the station to the boat and got on just about at 8.

A wind had come up and it looked bad outside. These boats have to go through a lock because the tides are so high.

The Bay of Fundy is the only place with tides higher than the Bristol Channel. Here the tides are from 30 to 45 feet.

A big Russian freighter was the first scheduled to go through the locks. He was empty (i.e., in ballast) (*weight carried at the bottom of a ship for stability*) as are we. Just as he was entering the locks a big gust of wind blew him against the wall. He stayed in the locks a long time examining the damage and it was 10:30 before he went on. The Maplewood was next through. However, it was then late, the wind high, and our ship light so the captain decided to wait for the next tide around tomorrow noon.

There is a big Spanish ship, the Atxeri-Mendi anchored close by that has been there for 2 years. There is some squabble about her as she is claimed both by Franco and the loyalists.[3]

To bed about 11.

We were warned not to walk on the front deck as the firemen are all so drunk they might be dangerous.

By this time, you are desperate to get home and will take whatever passage you can get even if the ship is empty. I notice how proactive you both are, going directly to the captain instead of waiting for him to arrive at the shipping company office.

This is your first mention of the situation in Spain, which is not on your itinerary. Throughout the fall of 1937 and into early 1938, news of the civil war in Spain and the war in China dominate the international pages of Time Magazine, which you like to read.

While the 1935 edition of *Hand-Me-Down* has 10 pages on Spain, the 1938 edition omits Spain, with this note: "Owing to the present conditions in Spain, we feel that any notes we might submit would be hopelessly erroneous if not entirely obsolete; therefore, until the situation changes, we deem it advisable to discontinue this section of the *Hand-Me-Down*." Full of hope, however, the editors request that travelers send them information on Spain in the future.

NOTES

1. Because Edward VII insisted on marrying Wallis Simpson, an American woman who was divorced and morally suspect in the eyes of the British public, he was forced to abdicate his throne in December 1936, and his brother became King George VI. In 1937, the former king and his wife, now the Duke and Duchess of Windsor, visited Germany as guests of Hitler and were thought to be Nazi sympathizers.

2. According to the Archives and Collection Society, Ontario, Canada, Willowpool was mined in 1939 and sank near Newarp Light Vessel off the coast of England.

3. In 1939, the Atxeri-Mendi was transferred from one shipping company to another (Naviera Aznar) and renamed Monte Isabela. On September 20, 1946, it struck a reef and sank near Las Palmas. www.theshipslist.com/ships/lines/aznar.htm

9

PASSAGE HOME

August 19

There was still a pretty good wind this morning and there was some talk of waiting until tonight before sailing. However, about 11 the captain decided all at once to go and we were out in the ocean before 12. I just had time to run down the ladder and take a picture.

The wind is straight from the west, but the swells are not too big. However, I knew I would not feel well long. I got rid of the first part of my supper, but kept the rest of it down.

August 20

Kinda sea sick.

August 21

Not much like Sunday except we had eggs for breakfast. The food has been better than on the Themisto, but according to the captain will not stay good long. The fresh meat lasts only 4 or 5 days and then comes the corned beef, etc.

The wind shifted a little to the "souwest" late at night.

August 22

Last night was awful. The wind came directly from the side and the rollers were big and all night long the ship went from side to side. This morning we were tired out from trying to hold ourselves in the bunks. The ship being empty rolls a lot more than a loaded one would. We knew this before we started but were anxious to get home. Now we are even more anxious to get home.

I know you are anxious to get home, and you were lucky to find this freighter going to Quebec. This will seem like a very long trip!

August 23

Same old story. Sea sickish and "souwest" winds.

August 24

Last night was the very worst we have had. The wind changed from "souwest" to west. However, the big long rollers still came from the side or were sort of mixed up by the change of wind. This morning M. and I felt about as bad as we have since starting.

However, about 2 o'clock the wind began to ease up a "wee bit" and the sea went down along toward evening. We began to feel better and I read some for the first time without making me feel bad. M. has been reading before.

After supper we listened to the captain talk about his experiences for a couple of hours. He is a regular old sailor and has lots of stories to tell. He seems to really enjoy a good bottle in a pub. Later we went to his room and had some good port wine and listened to him and his radio at the same time. He really seems well informed and there is no doubt about his knowledge of navigation.

To bed about 10:20.

I imagine the captain is happy to have the company of two young Americans who are good listeners and conversationalists, and also like to have a "good bottle in a pub." You must be reassured that he is so knowledgeable about navigation.

August 25

Last night we both had the best night's rest since coming aboard. The wind has gone down a great deal and there is no sea, but a long easy swell that brings the propeller out and keeps up back some. However our speed is around 9 knots.[1] From noon yesterday to noon today our calculated distance was 199 miles. We passed the 30° west line this morning and they say we can now expect better weather.

Breakfast this morning (not that I can talk about food) consisted of the usual oatmeal, bread, butter (very rancid), marmalade, tea, and then stewed kidneys in a gravy and mashed potatoes.

Lunch: split pea soup (good), corned beef or canned beef (choice), fried onions, cabbage, boiled potatoes, and a cranberry tart sort of thing. Of course bread, butter, etc. Coffee at dinner, tea at all other times.

My stomach was so good today I even visited the galley (*kitchen*) and had a long talk with the cook. Later went back to see the work the captain is doing in the storage room under the poop deck (*a deck above the upper deck at the stern*).

Supper: cod roe, potatoes, cold meat, pickled beets.

August 26

Did not sleep well last night, probably because of lack of exercise. Wind going down, but still a pretty good swell.

Eggs and bacon for breakfast.

They started painting the forward part of the ship today. Rain stopped them about 3.

The wind has shifted around to the "soweast" and is giving us a push. At one time we were going close to 12 knots and this is darned good. The water is smooth as a lake.

Tonight the captain took the first mate, M. and me to his cabin for drinks and a little chat.

August 27

The fog horn blew most of the night, but this morning the water was very smooth and the wind still boosting us along. The wheel on the log line (*the device for measuring a vessel's speed through the water*) just whirling around.

At noon we had made 244 miles since yesterday noon and they consider that excellent. They even began to talk about getting to Quebec by Thursday noon.

Helped the captain scrape paint from a ventilator and got a little exercise this morning.

However, all of our expectations for Thursday at Quebec were ruined this afternoon. The barometer fell very rapidly and a strong south wind came up and soon a heavy sea began to form and the ship to roll. Believe me this ship can roll, it was by far the worst we have had. I left the settee in the third mate's room just before a wet battery came crashing down from a shelf above. Was I lucky?

I did not feel particularly bad, but my stomach surely threw the stuff out. M. came around during my worst spell and told me to try not to strain so hard; I could have thrown *her* out.

Yes, you were so lucky! You might have been severely injured, or worse. It is wonderful for you, and for me, that this didn't happen.

In *The Freighter Travel Manual,* Angier Bradford writes about the prolonged blast a ship must sound at least every two minutes whenever there are weather conditions such as fog. He notes that it seems no one would get to sleep, but in fact the regular-ity of the sound has a somnolent effect such that many people never sleep better.

August 28

What a night! Thrown side to side all night long and no let up this morning. However, we took some pictures this morning that I hope will be good.

Both of us slept a little this morning after the rolling had let up a little. By 12 o'clock the wind had died down quite a bit and the sea was more quiet. By 2 it was fairly smooth and we were again making 8 knots or better. Now at 9 o'clock they say we are up to 9½ knots again.

Blair Athol

Fog settled down this afternoon though, but that does not seem to bother these fellows. They just put out a lookout and blow the horn and go full speed ahead.

Made only 147 miles to noon today.

August 29

This morning was nice and clear and very little wind. We were going right along and made 244 miles at noon.

There were two icebergs about 6 to 7 miles to starboard (*the right side of the ship*) this morning when we got up. One was quite large but the other only a growler (*a small iceberg*). Looked nice through the glasses but too far away for a picture.

Sited Belle Isle (*an island at the Eastern tip of Newfoundland, at the entrance to the Gulf of St. Lawrence*) about 10 this morning and passed the lower end (only a couple of hundred yards off) at 1:45. It was a bleak barren looking place.

This morning M. washed some clothes and her hair and I helped paint the ship. Have not been getting much exercise and was glad of the chance to do something.

Data:

Dimensions of Blair Athol:

340'- 2" x 48'- 6" x 25'- 0"

340'- 2" BT x 48'- 6" BM x 25'- 0" DM

Water Ballast	1,235 tons
Bunkers	1,678
Dead weight	5,600
Gross tonnage	3,319
Net tonnage	2,005

Dead weight of ship is actual weight of ship + cargo + water + bunkers (*large bins for the stowage of coal aboard ship*), etc. Gross tonnage is measurement of *volume* (not weight) of everything. Net tonnage is gross tonnage minus all space used for accommodations, such as wheel house, engine room, etc.

Distance Port Talbot to Quebec:

Port Talbot to Helwick Light Vessel[2]	24 miles
H. Lt. V. to St. Govans Lt. V.	23
St. G. to Fastnet[3]	174
Fastnet to Belle Isle	1,681
Belle Isle to Father Pt.	562
Father Pt. To Quebec	158
	2,622

As we came along Belle Isle we could see some peaks on Newfoundland to the south. Then the Coast of Labrador was very clearly visible to the north as soon as we got past the end of Belle Isle.

Just like a mathematician! Here you show your true colors: like the scholar you are, you have a mini-research project going on, and now you are compiling the data. But how do you obtain all of this information, and what are your sources? Perhaps the captain shares his extensive knowledge with you. Your journal entries throughout this passage home show your interest in keeping track of the ship's speed and distance traveled. Why should I be surprised? You just spent two years at Princeton studying measure theory, and here you get a chance to "measure" aspects of your travel.

August 30

[No entry]

August 31

This was the most beautiful day imaginable. The sun shone all day, there was only a slight breeze, and the water was as smooth and calm as could be. We sat out on deck chairs a lot.

This afternoon I took a couple of pictures of old flat feet (*captain and officers*) and then went into the focsle (*fo'c's'le—forecastle, the crew's quarters*) to see where the sailors and crew live. It is a very dingy dirty place and small. The bunks had dirty blankets and the fellows on night duty were lying there trying to sleep while the others were talking. There is a stove and a moveable little table where they ate. As soon as the firemen come off of duty they go right to bed. They seem to get up only long enough to eat and work.

The evening was cool and invigorating and there was a beautiful sunset.

September 1

The pilot came on board at 2:30 last night at Father Point (*Point-au-Père*). It was rainy and foggy at the time and was a continuous downpour until about 9 o'clock. The fog or rain did not slow them down any though, they just plowed right on through. Later it cleared off though and the hills close by were very pretty.

The river narrows down more than I remembered it so the shores are close. We were running against the tide from about 10 until 4 or 5. At one place the water flows 5 or 6 knots so our speed was considerably reduced. They speeded the engines up a little to compensate though.

[Notes in back of notebook on different ships, distances, names and addresses of people met, purchases of tweed material, pipe, paper, soap, liqueur, chocolates, mints, fruit.]

Your journal ends here. How typical of you to end in such a matter-of-fact manner. I guess you have had enough of writing and now want to concentrate on getting home. Perhaps the journey seems over at this point. But I certainly would have liked to read about your reaching Quebec and saying goodbye to the captain and crew. I would have liked to read some final words about your trip now that it is over. Instead, as is true throughout this project, I have to accept the empty spaces in your journal and fill in where I can.

Fortunately, I have found clues to what happened next and where my parents went after arriving at Quebec. I assumed they would go right back to Ithaca since my father resumed teaching at Cornell after the two years at Princeton. His "expenses notebook," which I found much later confirms this. The entry for September 2 lists these expenses:

Taxi	.45	Tobacco	.66
Bus, Quebec to Montreal	8.50	Supper	.74
Lunch	.32	Movie	.50
Room	1.50	Car Storage	13.00
Tram	.07		

Now I know they took a bus from Quebec to Montreal, where they had stored their car during the three months they were in Europe. So what about that short story my father wrote in 1949 in which my brother, the narrator, says his parents hitchhiked to Quebec? Now I think perhaps they hitchhiked from Montreal (not Ithaca) to Quebec at the beginning of the trip. From there they sailed to Holland on the SS Themisto, a Dutch freighter operated by Zeevaart Lines in Rotterdam.

Even better, I also found a postcard that my mother wrote to friends in Syracuse, New York, dated August 14, 1938. She often asked people to save her postcards and give them to her when she returned from trips. This one was addressed to Dr. and Mrs. A.D. Campbell; Alan Ditchfield Campbell was an associate professor of mathematics at Syracuse University.[4]

In it, she wrote: "We've had a grand time and are now waiting to sail—we should be on our way now but we're having trouble with the Canadian Travel League. We hope to sail this week from Swansea (we are waiting for a telegram and will go immediately by ferry from Ilfracombe). We will see you on our way from Montreal to Ithaca."

A grand time! How good it is to read this. While your journal contains some expressions of delight, they are few and far between. This may be the difference between writing a postcard and writing a trip journal, but it also reveals differences between the two of you—she more outgoing and you more reserved.

Knowing now that the summer of 1938 was the last opportunity for Americans to travel abroad easily for at least seven years, I am grateful that my parents took this trip and that they were able to get passage home in time. By the end of September, Americans will be urged to leave Europe, and in early November, Kristallnacht will bring changes that we still live with today.

NOTES

1. One knot is the speed of one nautical mile per hour or 1.15 land miles.

2. A light vessel is a ship that serves as a lighthouse, with a light on a very tall mast. Listed here are two light vessels passed by on the passage from Wales: Helwick and St. Govans.

3. Fastnet Rock, a high rock about four and a half miles south of Ireland, with a lighthouse.

4. On January 8, 1936, A.D. Campbell wrote a letter to Oswald Veblen in support of John Randolph's application to the Institute for Advanced Study for the year 1936-37. He wrote, "He has both the urge and the ability to produce research work of high quality. His published papers show this." He went on to cite having gone on camping trips with him to the Adirondacks many times. (Records of the School of Mathematics, Member Files, 1933–1977, The Shelby White and Leon Levy Archives Center, Institute for Advanced Study, Princeton, NJ)

Note: At the back of one notebook, my father wrote the following observations:

Incidents

In Rotterdam the people in apartments above shops have mirrors mounted outside their windows in such a way that when they sit in their easy chairs they can see people coming down the street.

The Belgian train conductor who called two women to move their bags six inches so he could go through a door more easily.

The English girls offering us free use of their bicycles to go from London to Swansea before they even knew our names.

In Bruges, the Englishman staying at the Pension "buyed a grapefruit" and wanted "to see a chapie down the street who has a row boat I want to buy" and "by-byed" us after our first talk with him.

In Rudesheim M. (knowing no German and a little French) talking French to a little German boy (knowing no English and a little French).

In Donaueschingen, the German taking Coca Cola after his meal. It was served, bottle and wine glass, on a little tray.

In Baden-Baden, we talked to a man and asked him for a good place to get a beer. He recommended a place very highly; even said that beer at other places was no good. We later went to the place and found that he worked there.

The time in Bruges we walked out to look at the natives, but the natives looked at us because M. had on her rain cape.

AFTERWORD

World War II began one year later. On September 1, 1939, Germany invaded Poland, and two days later France and England declared war on Germany. My parents, safely home in Ithaca, New York, must have talked about the timing of their trip to Europe as the war began and countries they had visited were invaded — and in the years to come, as the terrible events unfolded and more became known about the Holocaust.

But, again, I don't know this for sure. There is little I know with certainty even after following their trip so closely and asking so many questions about its context and details. What I do know is that my father's recording of their trip every day became a gift to me. The decision to write back to my father allowed me to re-imagine my parents—to see them with new eyes as an adult though still a daughter—and to link part of their lives to history. I am grateful that through this work I have been able to witness their spirit, their creativity, their resilience, and their courage to experience the world beyond the confines of the United States. I came to feel connected to my young parents in a way that never would have been possible otherwise.

I was fortunate to find the four small notebooks that constituted a journal, the two notebooks with lists of expenses, the postcards, the photographs my father took, my mother's youth hostel card, and the walking stick from Switzerland. Such documents and objects afford a glimpse into daily life in Europe as witnessed, and experienced, by these two young Americans. Not satisfied with only a glimpse, I tried to find a larger view, to see beyond what they saw at the time. I hope this attempt has opened the window a little bit more on that critical time in history—the summer of 1938.

JOHN F. RANDOLPH: PROFILE

JOHN ADAM FITZ RANDOLPH was born in Newton, Iowa on May 2, 1904. When his mother Carrie died of tuberculosis in 1913, his father Albert Clyde moved the family of four children from place to place, trying out new ideas and inventions, and eventually remarrying and settling in California in 1920.

Albert Clyde Randolph was ingenious, enterprising, and athletic. As a young adult, he invented a rice threshing machine in Louisiana and built an electric light plant and cotton gin in Palacios, Texas, a fishing port on the Gulf of Mexico. Foreseeing that the automobile would force the horse and buggy off the road, he opened the first garage and car repair shop in Colorado Springs. In 1927, working for Ryan Aircraft in San Diego, he conceived of and installed the periscope (aeroscope) that was so useful to Charles Lindbergh in the Spirit of St. Louis. In his later years, even into his eighties, he kept in shape by working out with weights.

When John Randolph was fifteen years old, he left home in California to help his aunt and uncle with the summer harvest in the Texas Panhandle. He thrived on the hard, physical life of rural Texas and never returned home to his father and stepmother. After two years, his aunt and uncle moved to California, but he stayed behind, and several families in the community took him in for weeks at a time. Eventually, working for a cattle rancher while going to school, he earned enough money to buy a horse and a cow with the goal of having his own ranch one day.

He rode the horse to school—a one-room schoolhouse in Ochiltree County—but he never became a rancher. Fortunately for him, the young woman responsible for teaching grades one through twelve knew nothing about mathematics. Required to learn plane geometry if he wanted to graduate from high school, he taught himself from a book in the evenings. He passed on what he had learned to the one other student at his level. This experience, which combined mathematics and teaching, changed the direction of his life.

In 1922, he graduated from high school, sold his horse and cow, and with these earnings enrolled in West Texas State Teachers College (now West Texas A&M University) in Canyon. He majored in mathematics, played softball, tennis, and piccolo in the band, and was president of the college press club in his senior year. After graduating in 1926, he taught mathematics in the high school in Canyon for one year and went on to earn his master's degree in mathematics from the University of Michigan in 1928. His first college teaching job was at Syracuse University, where he met Margaret Crowley, a student there; they were married in 1932.

In 1934, he earned his Ph.D. in mathematics and astronomy from Cornell University in Ithaca, New York, and then taught there until 1943, except for two years (1936-38). He was professor of mathematics at Oberlin College from 1943 to 1948 and spent the next twenty-one years at the University of Rochester, where he was Fayerweather Professor and chaired the Mathematics Department in the nineteen fifties. He also taught at the American University of Beirut during sabbatical leaves in the fifties and sixties. After retiring from the University of Rochester, he was Visiting Distinguished Professor at the Rochester Institute of Technology. He wrote seven college mathematics textbooks; he was working on his eighth when he died in 1988. His spirit lives on today in the John F. Randolph Lecture in mathematics education, established for the Seaway Section of the Mathematical Association of America.

In May 1938, John Randolph had just spent two years as a member at the Institute for Advanced Study in Princeton, New Jersey. Abraham Flexner, founding director, envisioned the Institute in 1931 as a haven where scholars and scientists would have the freedom to pursue intellectual inquiry where it led them without the constraints of teaching or other obligations. John and Margaret lived at 43 Linden Lane in Princeton.

By the late thirties, an amazing mathematical community was flourishing at the Institute.* Albert Einstein was there, along with Oswald Veblen and John von Neumann, who would develop the early theory of electronic computers. Already foreseeing a difficult climate in his home country, Einstein had left Germany in 1933 and accepted a position at the newly created Institute in Princeton, where he remained until 1955. Years later, John Randolph would recall noticing Einstein's mismatched socks (on the few occasions that he wore socks).

In his copy of the now classic *Men of Mathematics* by E.T. Bell, John Randolph had folded within its pages a review of the book from the *New York Times Book Review* section, dated April 11, 1937. The reviewer praises E.T. Bell for "seeking an appreciation of abstractness and generality, a comprehension of the faith of mathematics in itself and its ability to create human values, and an understanding of why we are at present living in the Golden Age of Mathematics." That the Golden Age was flourishing at the Institute for Advanced Study was apparent then and is remembered today with affection and respect.

In a letter of recommendation dated September 23, 1940, Marston Morse wrote, "Recently [Randolph] spent two years at the Institute for Advanced Study under a stipend granted

---

* In one of the "expenses" notebooks from the trip, Margaret Randolph wrote a list of names with a check mark next to each. Most likely, this was a list of the people she sent postcards to from Europe. In addition to family members, the names read like a "who's who" of mathematicians in the late thirties: Veblens (Oswald Veblen), Weyls (Hermann Weyl), Tuckers (Albert Tucker), Durens (William L. Duren), Marston Morse, Gordon Fullers, Flexners (most likely William W. Flexner), Gillespie (David C. Gillespie), Morses (Anthony P. Morse), and also Miss Blake (Gwen Blake, the Institute for Advanced Study's School of Mathematics secretary).

by the Institute. We were much impressed by him here, not only by his scholarship, but also by his mathematical insight and ability to penetrate to the bottom of difficult problems.... He is particularly adapted for a position as head of a department because he is deliberate in nature, fair, kindly and sympathetic." He also offered, "Both Mr. and Mrs. Randolph are most agreeable and charming, and have made friends wherever they have been." (Records of the School of Mathematics, Member Files, 1933–1977, The Shelby White and Leon Levy Archives Center, Institute for Advanced Study)

Upon leaving Princeton in May 1938, and before returning to academic life at Cornell, John and Margaret Randolph set out for Europe on a freighter. He had just turned 34 years old, and she was 27. Every day, from May 28 to September 1, 1938, he wrote about their experiences in four small notebooks (3½ "x 6"). He wrote his entries in pencil, in his tiny but legible handwriting. The notebooks appeared among his papers after his death. Other documents and a number of photographs from the trip have turned up over the years.

JOHN F. RANDOLPH: PUBLICATIONS

Books

Analytic Geometry and Calculus (with Mark Kac). New York: Macmillan, 1946.

Primer of College Mathematics. New York: Macmillan, 1950.

Calculus. New York: Macmillan, 1952.

Trigonometry. New York: Macmillan, 1953.

Calculus and Analytic Geometry. Belmont, CA: Wadsworth Publishing Company, 1963.

Calculus, Analytic Geometry, Vectors. Belmont, CA: Dickenson, 1967.

Basic Real and Abstract Analysis. New York and London: Academic Press, 1968.

Journal Articles

"Vector Methods as a Basis for Mathematical Formulation of the Data of Genothera Genetics." *Michigan Academy of Science* (1931).

"Concerning Measure and Linear Density Properties of Point Sets." *Bulletin of the American Mathematical Society* 39 (1933): 873–874.

"Carathéodory Measure and a Generalization of the Gauss-Green Lemma." *Bulletin of the American Mathematical Society* 40 (1934): 793.

"Carathéodory Measure and a Generalization of the Gauss-Green Lemma." *Transactions of the American Mathematical Society* 38 (1935): 531–548.

"Some Density Properties of Point Sets." *Bulletin of the American Mathematical Society* 41 (1935): 202.

"On Generalizations of Length and Area." *Bulletin of the American Mathematical Society* 41 (1935): 623.

"On Generalizations of Length and Area." *Bulletin of the American Mathematical Society* 42 (1936): 268–274.

"Some Density Properties of Point Sets." *Annals of Mathematics* 37 (1936): 336–344.

"Carathédory Linear Measure and Vitali's Theorem." *Bulletin of the American Mathematical Society* 42 (1936): 34.

"The Vitali Covering Theorem for Carathéodory Linear Measure." *Annals of Mathematics* 40 (April 1939): 299–308.

"Metric Separability and Outer Integrals." *Bulletin of the American Mathematical Society* 46 (1940): 934– 939.

"Distances Between Points of the Cantor Set." *American Mathematical Monthly* 47 (1940): 549–551.

"Gillespie Measure" (with Anthony P. Morse). *Duke Mathematical Journal* 6 (June 1940): 408–419.

"Some Properties of Sets of the Cantor Type." *Journal of the London Mathematical Society* 16 (1941): 38– 42.

"Differentials" (with Mark Kac). *American Mathematical Monthly* 49 (Feb. 1942): 110–112.

"The φ Rectifiable Subsets of the Plane" (with Anthony P. Morse). *Transactions of the American Mathematical Society* 55 (1944): 236–305.

"Gillespie Measure" (with Anthony P. Morse). *Fundamenta Mathematicae* 33 (1945): 12–26.

"A Polynomial Counter." *IEEE Transactions on Electronic Computers* 12 (1963): 320.

"Cross-Examining Propositional Calculus and Set Operations." *American Mathematical Monthly* 72 (Feb. 1965): 117–127.

"Corrections for 'Cross-Examining Propositional Calculus and Set Operations.'" *American Mathematical Monthly* 72 (Aug.–Sept. 1965): 739.

"Psycho-Logics: An Axiomatic System Describing Human Behavior" (with C.A. Hilgartner). *Journal of Theoretical Biology* 23 (May 1969): 285–338.

"Psycho-Logics: 2. The Structure of 'Unimpaired' Human Behavior" (with C.A. Hilgartner). *Journal of Theoretical Biology* 23 (June 1969): 347–374.

"Psycho-Logics: 3. The Structure of Empathy" (with C.A. Hilgartner). *Journal of Theoretical Biology* 24 (July 1969): 1–29.

Reviews

Hardy, G.H. "A Mathematician's Apology." *American Mathematical Monthly* 49 (Jun.–Jul., 1942): 396–397.

Raghavachari, T.K. "An Introduction to Analytical Geometry and Calculus." *American Mathematical Monthly* 49 (Aug.–Sep., 1942): 469–470.

Cell, J.W. "Engineering Problems Illustrating Mathematics." *American Mathematical Monthly* 51 (May, 1944): 280.

REFERENCES

Abzug, Robert H. *America Views the Holocaust 1933–1945*. Boston: Bedford/St. Martin's, 1999.

Angier, Bradford. *The Freighter Travel Manual*. Radnor, PA: Chilton Book Co., 1974.

Baker, Nicholson. *Human Smoke: The Beginnings of World War II, the End of Civilization*. New York: Simon and Schuster, 2008.

Basu, Shrabani. *Spy Princess: The Life of Noor Inayat Khan*. New Lebanon, NY: Omega Publications, 2007.

Bernstein, Mark, and Alex Lubertozzi. *World War II on the Air: Edward R. Murrow and the Broadcasts that Riveted a Nation*. Naperville, IL: Sourcebooks, Inc., 2003.

Bessel, Richard. *Life in the Third Reich*. Oxford: Oxford University Press, 2001.

Breitman, Richard. *Official Secrets: What the Nazis Planned, What the British and Americans Knew*. New York: Hill and Wang, 1998.

Brettell, Caroline B. *Writing Against the Wind: A Mother's Life History*. Wilmington, DE: Scholarly Resources, Inc., 1999.

Burrows, Carlyle. "Notes and Comments on Events in Art." *New York Herald Tribune* (November 21, 1937): VII 9.

Campbell, A.D., "Advice to the Graduate Assistant." *American Mathematical Monthly,* 45 (January 1938): 32–33.

DePauli, Werner, and John L. Casti. *Godel: A Life of Logic*. Cambridge, MA: Perseus Publishing, 2001.

Evans, Richard J. *The Third Reich in Power: 1933–1939*. New York: Penguin Books, 2005.

Flexner, Abraham. *An Autobiography*. New York: Simon and Schuster, 1960.

Freedman, Samuel G. *Who She Was: My Search for My Mother's Life*. New York: Simon and Schuster, 2005.

Friedlander, Saul. *Nazi Germany and the Jews: Vol. 1. The Years of Persecution, 1933–1939*. New York: HarperCollins, 1997.

Fry, Varian. *Surrender on Demand*. New York: Random House, 1945.

Fuller, Jean Overton. *Noor-un-nisa Inayat Khan*. London and The Hague: East-West Publications, 1971.

Gay, Peter. *My German Question: Growing up in Nazi Berlin.* New Haven: Yale University Press, 1998.

Gilbert, Martin. *Auschwitz and the Allies.* New York: Henry Holt, 1981.

_____. *Kristallnacht: Prelude to Destruction.* New York: HarperCollins, 2006.

Glaborson, William. "For Betrayal by Bank and Nazis, $21 Million," *New York Times,* April 14, 2005, sec. A.

Gorra, Michael. *The Bells in Their Silence: Travels Through Germany.* Princeton, NJ: Princeton University Press, 2004.

Guerin, Daniel. *The Brown Plague.* Durham, NC: Duke University Press, 1994.

Hamburger, Philip. "Letter from Berchtesgaden," *The New Yorker* (June 9, 1945): 51-55.

Hampl, Patricia. *I Could Tell You Stories: Sojourn in the Land of Memory.* New York: W.W. Norton, 1999.

Herbert, Bob. "Acts of Quiet Courage," *New York Times* (April 11, 2005): A.19.

Herlihy, David. V. *Bicycle: The History.* New Haven: Yale University Press, 2004.

Hegi, Ursula. *Stones From the River.* New York: Scribner, 1994.

Holocaust Claims Processing Office, New York State Banking Department. "Paintings Returned to Heirs of Holocaust Victims." Press release, Governor George E. Pataki, November 17, 2001. www.claims.state.ny.us/pr011127.htm.

Independent Commission of Experts Switzerland—Second World War. *Switzerland, National Socialism and the Second World War: Final Report.* Zürich: Pendo Editions, 2002.

Jerome, Jerome K. *Three Men in a Boat and Three Men on the Bummel.* London: Penguin Books, 1999.

Johnson, Eric A., and Karl-Heinz Reuband. *What We Knew: Terror, Mass Murder, and Everyday Life in Nazi Germany.* London: John Murray Publishers, 2005.

Kac, Mark. *Enigmas of Chance: An Autobiography.* New York: Harper and Row, 1985.

Kaplan, Marion A. *Between Dignity and Despair: Jewish Life in Nazi Germany.* Oxford: Oxford University Press, 1998.

Kater, Michael H. *Hitler Youth.* Cambridge, MA: Harvard University Press, 2004.

Klemperer, Victor. *I Will Bear Witness, 1933–1941: A Diary of the Nazi Years*. New York: Modern Library, 1999.

Laqueur, Walter. *The Terrible Secret: Suppression of the Truth About Hitler's "Final Solution."* New York: Henry Holt, 1980.

Leff, Laurel. *Buried by the Times: The Holocaust and America's Most Important Newspaper*. Cambridge: Cambridge University Press, 2005.

Liebling, A.J. *The Road Back to Paris*. New York: Random House, Modern Library Edition, 1997 (orig. 1944).

_____. *The Sweet Science*. New York: Penguin Books, 1982 (orig. 1956).

Lipstadt, Deborah E. *Beyond Belief: The American Press and the Coming of the Holocaust 1933–1945*. New York: Free Press, 1986.

Luick-Thrams, Aliza Michael. "Documenting My 'Neighbor's' Fate," *Friends Journal* (June 2007): 6-9, 40.

Lukacs, John. *Five Days in London: May 1940*. New Haven, CT: Yale University Press, 1999.

Metelmann, Henry. *A Hitler Youth: Growing Up in Germany in the 1930s*. Staplehurst, UK: Spellmount, 2004.

Morris, Wright. *Solo, An American Dreamer in Europe: 1933–1934*. New York: Harper and Row, 1983.

Morrison, Blake. *Things My Mother Never Told Me*. New York: Granta Books, 2002.

Némirovsky, Irène. *Suite Française*. New York: Vintage Books, 2007.

New York Times, "Austria Paying for Nazis' Forced Labor, to Mixed Emotions," October 16, 2003, B2.

Nixon, Larry. *Vagabond Voyaging: The Story of Freighter Travel*. Boston: Little, Brown, 1938.

Office of the United States Chief Counsel for Prosecution of Axis Criminality. *Nazi Conspiracy and Aggression,* vol. IV, doc. no. 1721-PS. Washington, DC: U.S. Government Printing Office, 1946.

Parssinen, Terry. *The Oster Conspiracy of 1938*. New York: HarperCollins, 2003.

Pickett, Clarence E. *For More than Bread: An Autobiographical Account of Twenty-Two Years' Work with the American Friends Service Committee*. Boston: Little, Brown, 1953.

Regis, Ed. *Who Got Einstein's Office? Eccentricity and Genius at the Institute for Advanced Study*. Reading, MA: Addison-Wesley, 1988.

Roth, Joseph. "The Myth of the German Soul," *Report from a Parisian Paradise: Essays from France, 1925–1939*. New York: Norton, 2004.

Segal, Sanford L. *Mathematicians under the Nazis*. Princeton, NJ: Princeton University Press, 2003.

Shirer, William L. *The Nightmare Years: 1930–1940*. Boston: Little, Brown, 1984.

Shriver, Donald W. *Honest Patriots: Loving a Country Enough to Remember Its Misdeeds*. New York: Oxford University Press, 2005.

Spector, Shmuel, ed. *The Encyclopedia of Jewish Life Before and During the Holocaust*. New York: New York University Press, 2001.

Stern, Fritz. *Five Germanys I have Known*. New York: Farrar, Straus and Giroux, 2006.

Student Tourist Class Association. *Hand-Me-Down: The Student Guide of Europe*. New York: Holland-America Line, 1935 and 1938.

Tank, Betty. *Pushing My Shadow: A Memoir 1939–1945*. Chatham Center, NY: Lily, 1995.

Time, "Optimist," June 27, 1938, 16-19.

_____, "Hitler Comes Home," March 21, 1938, 18-19.

Ulrich, Laurel Thatcher. *A Midwife's Tale*. New York: Vintage Books, 1991.

van Leer, Wim. *Time of My Life*. Jerusalem: Carta and Jerusalem Post, 1984.

Welch, David. *Propaganda and the German Cinema 1933–1945*. Oxford: Clarendon Press, 1983.

Yivo Institute for Jewish Research. "Otto Frank File Found at YIVO." Press Release, February 14, 2007.

Breinigsville, PA USA
15 August 2010
243632BV00001B/2/P